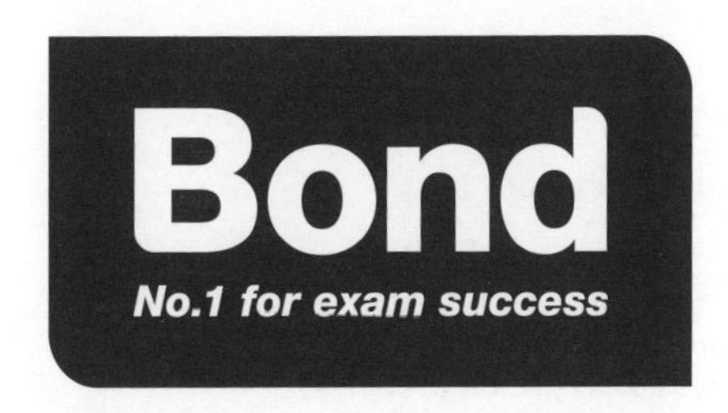

Non-verbal Reasoning

Assessment Papers

11+–12+ years

Book 2

Great Clarendon Street, Oxford, OX2 6DP, United Kingdom

Oxford University Press is a department of the University of Oxford. It furthers the University's objective of excellence in research, scholarship, and education by publishing worldwide. Oxford is a registered trade mark of Oxford University Press in the UK and in certain other countries

First published in 2015

British Library Cataloguing in Publication Data
Data available

978-0-19-274029-8

14

Paper used in the production of this book is a natural, recyclable product made from wood grown in sustainable forests.
The manufacturing process conforms to the environmental regulations of the country of origin..

Printed in China

Acknowledgements

The publishers would like to thank the following for permissions to use copyright material:

Page make-up: Wearset Ltd
Illustrations: Bede Illustration
Cover illustrations: Lo Cole

Although we have made every effort to trace and contact all copyright holders before publication this has not been possible in all cases. If notified, the publisher will rectify any errors or omissions at the earliest opportunity.

Before you get started

What is Bond?

This book is part of the Bond Assessment Papers series for non-verbal reasoning, which provides a **thorough and progressive course in non-verbal reasoning** from ages six to twelve. It builds up non-verbal reasoning skills from book to book over the course of the series. Bond's non-verbal reasoning resources are ideal preparation for the 11+ and other secondary school selection exams.

How does the scope of this book match real exam content?

Non-verbal Reasoning 11–12+ years Book 1 and *Book 2* are the advanced Bond 11+ books. Each paper is **pitched at a level above a typical 11+ exam,** providing greater challenges and stretching skills further. The papers practise a wide range of questions drawn from the four distinct groups of non-verbal reasoning question types: identifying shapes, missing shapes, rotating shapes, coded shapes and logic. The papers are fully in line with 11+ and other selective exams for this age group but are designed to practise **a wider variety of skills and question types** than most other practice papers so that children are always challenged to think – and don't get bored repeating the same question type again and again. We believe that variety is the key to effective learning. It helps children 'think on their feet' and cope with the unexpected: it is surprising how often children come out of non-verbal reasoning exams having met question types they have not seen before.

What does the book contain?

- **6 papers** – each one contains 60 questions.
- **Tutorial links throughout** – – this icon appears next to the questions. It indicates links to the relevant section in *How to do 11+ Non-verbal Reasoning*, our invaluable subject guide that offers explanations and practice for all core question types.
- **Scoring devices** – there is a score box at the end of each test and a Progress Chart on page 68. The chart is a visual and motivating way for children to see how they are doing. It also turns the score into a percentage that can help you decide what to do next.
- **Next Steps Planner** – advice on what to do after finishing the papers can be found on the inside back cover.
- **Answers** – located in an easily-removed central pull-out section.

How can you use this book?

One of the great strengths of Bond Assessment Papers is their flexibility. They can be used at home, in school and by tutors to:

- set **timed formal practice** tests – allow about 45 minutes per paper in line with standard 11^+ demands. Reduce the suggested time limit by five minutes to practise working at speed
- provide **bite-sized chunks** for regular practice
- **highlight strengths and weaknesses** in the core skills
- identify **individual needs**
- set **homework**
- follow **a complete 11 preparation strategy** alongside *The Parents' Guide to the* 11^+ (see below).

It is best to start at the beginning and work through the papers in order. If you are using the book as part of a careful run-in to the 11^+, we suggest that you also have two other essential Bond resources close at hand:

How to do 11^+ *Non-verbal Reasoning*: the subject guide that explains all the question types practised in this book. Use the cross-reference icons to find the relevant sections.

The Parents' Guide to the 11^+: the step-by-step guide to the whole 11^+ experience. It clearly explains the 11^+ process, provides guidance on how to assess children, helps you to set complete action plans for practice and explains how you can use the *Non-verbal Reasoning 11–*12^+ *years Book 1* and *Book 2* as part of a strategic run-in to the exam.

See the inside front cover for more details of these books.

What does a score mean and how can it be improved?

It is unfortunately impossible to predict how a child will perform when it comes to the 11^+ (or similar) exam if they achieve a certain score on any practice book or paper. Success on the day depends on a host of factors, including the scores of the other children sitting the test. However, we can give some guidance on what a score indicates and how to improve it.

If children colour in the Progress Chart on page 68, this will give an idea of present performance in percentage terms. The Next Steps Planner inside the back cover will help you to decide what to do next to help a child progress. It is always valuable to go over wrong answers with children. If they are having trouble with any particular question type, follow the tutorial links to *How to do* 11^+ *Non-verbal Reasoning* for step-by-step explanations and further practice.

Don't forget the website . . . !

Visit www.bond11plus.co.uk for lots of advice, information and suggestions on everything to do with Bond, the 11^+ and helping children to do their best.

Paper 1

B 4 Which one comes next? Circle the letter.

Example

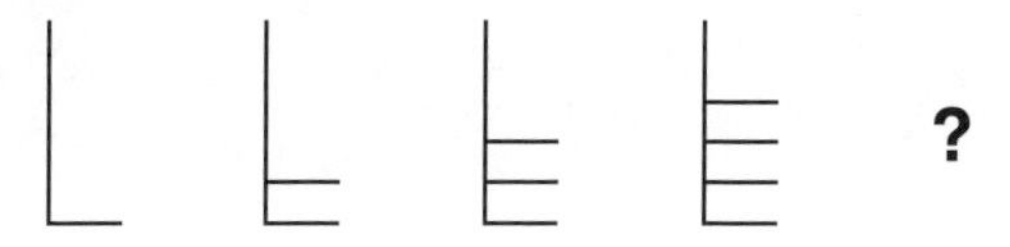 ?

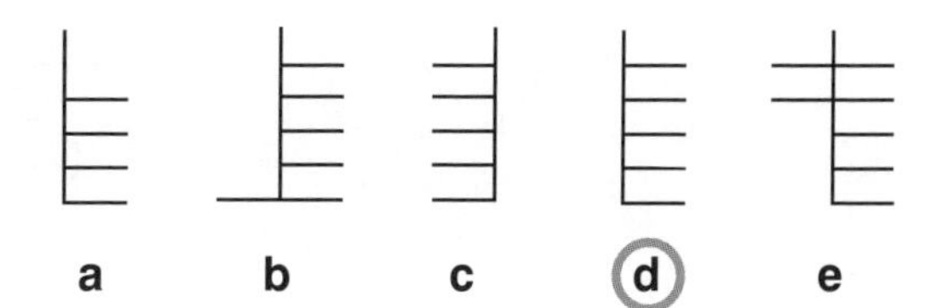

a b c **d** e

 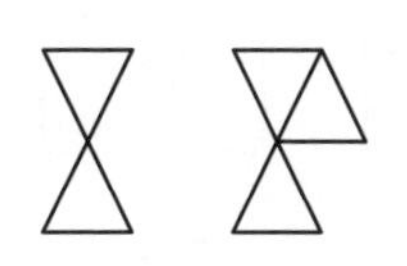 ? 

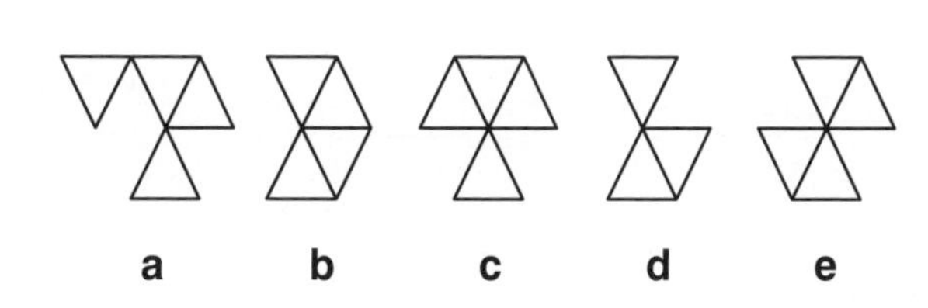

a b c d e

 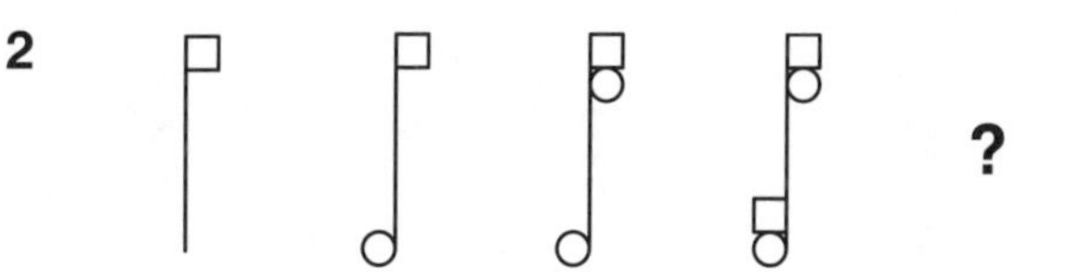 ?

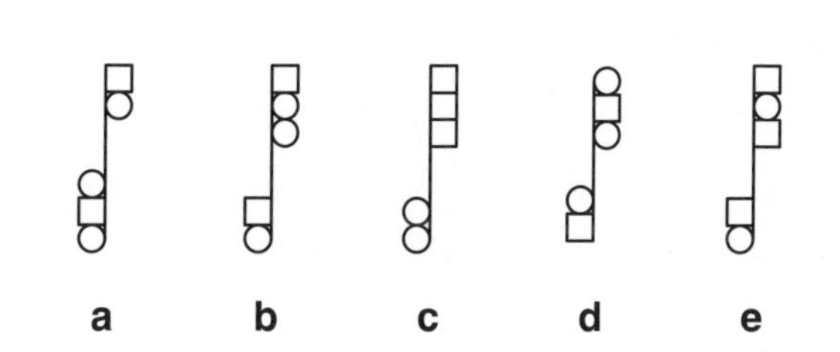

a b c d e

 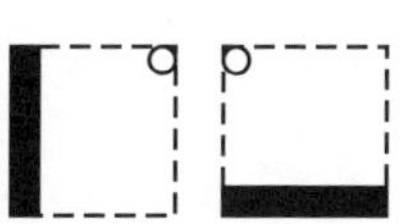 ? 

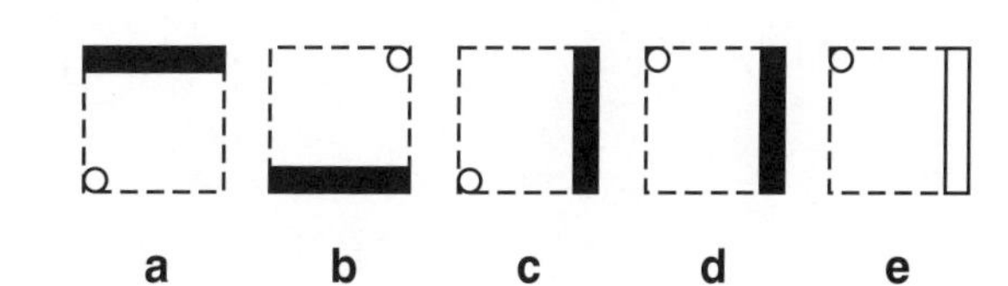

a b c d e

 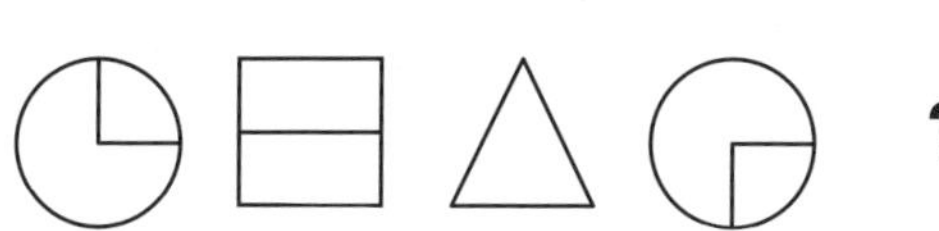 ?

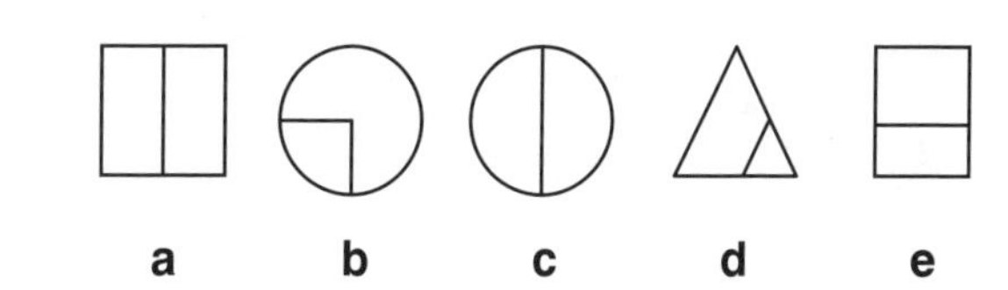

a b c d e

5 ?

a b c d e

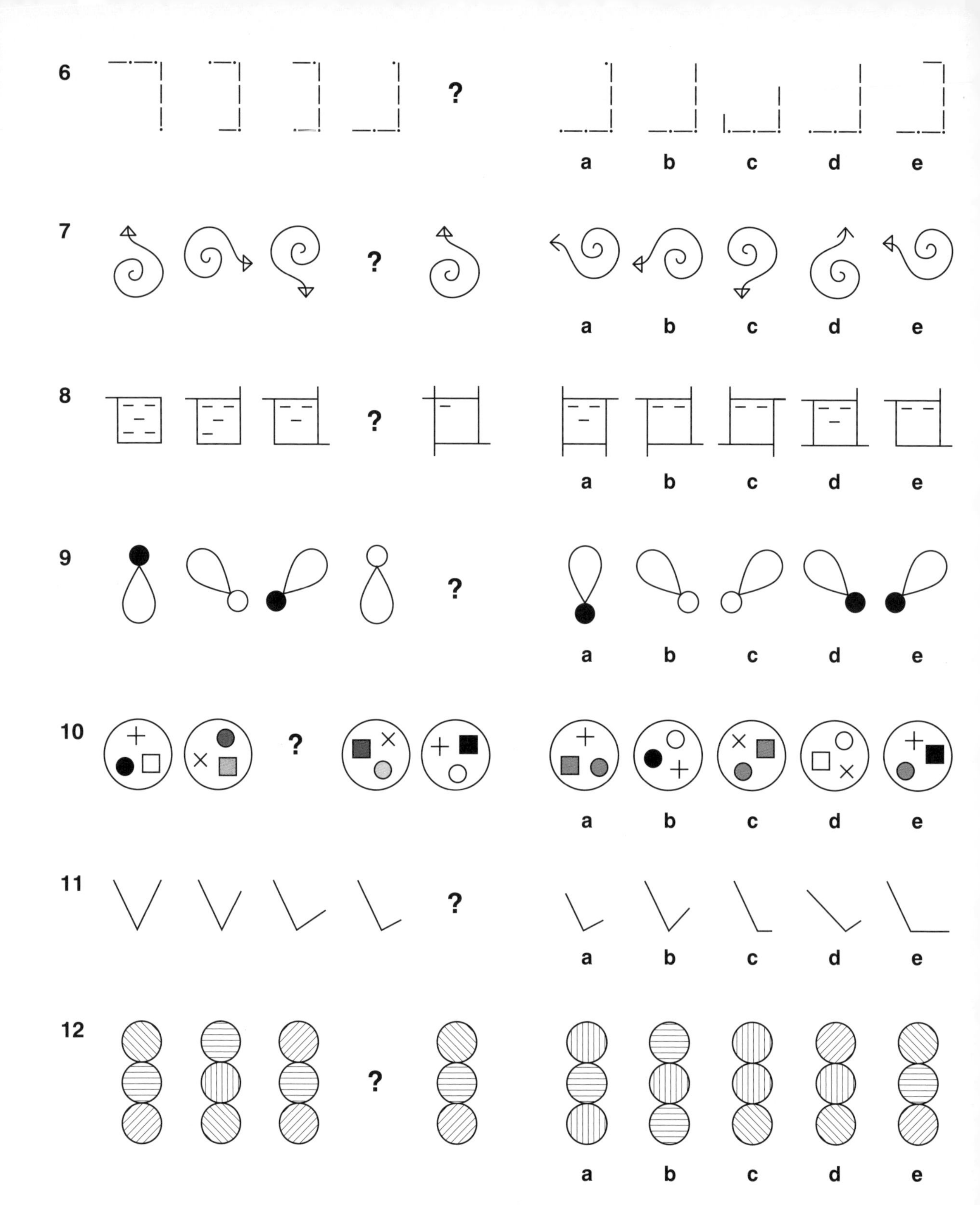
6
?
a
b
c
d
e
7
?
a
b
c
d
e
8
?
a
b
c
d
e
9
?
a
b
c
d
e
10
?
a
b
c
d
e
11
?
a
b
c
d
e
12
?
a
b
c
d
e

B7 Which shape on the right is the reflection of the shape given on the left? Circle the letter.

Example

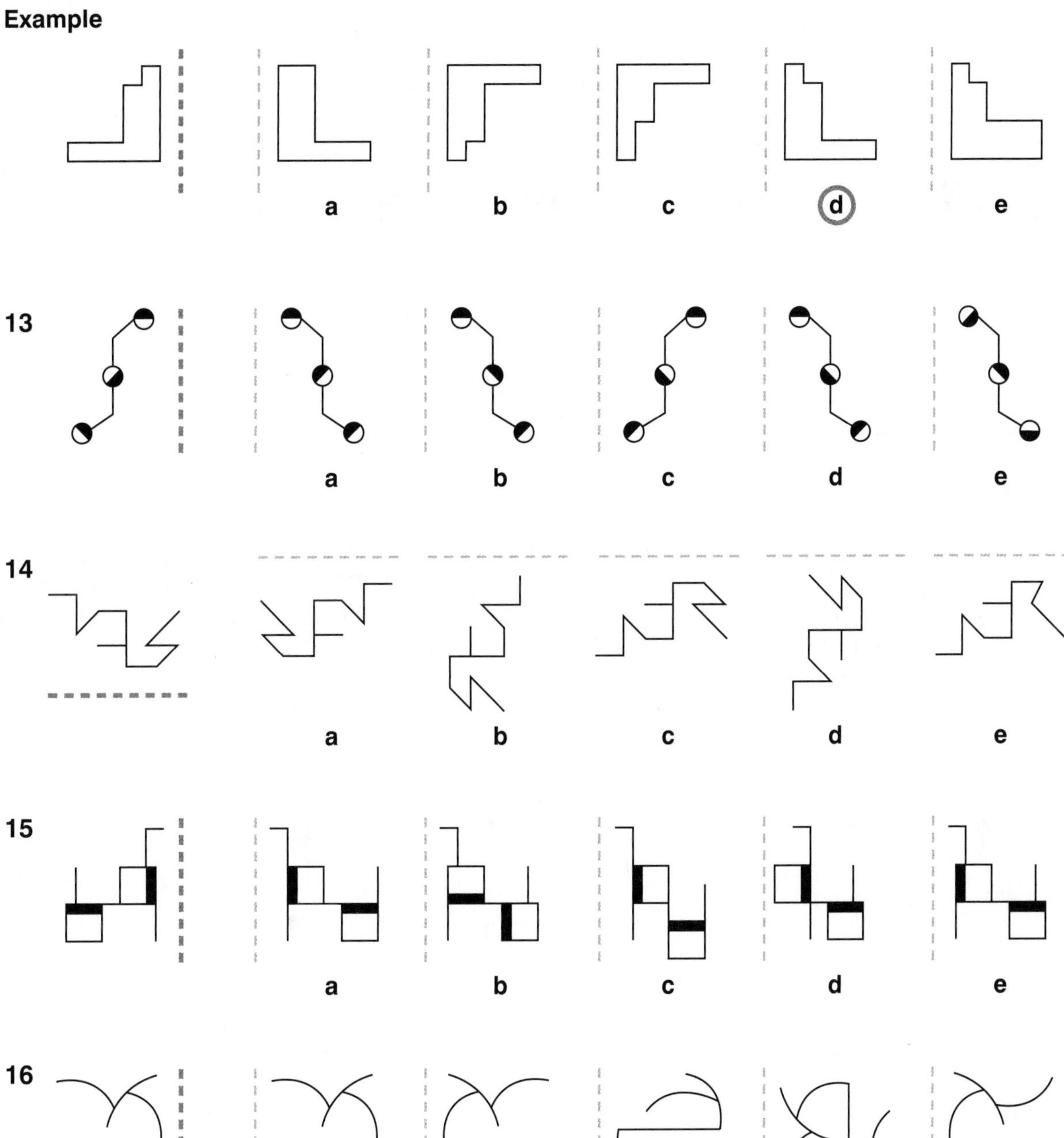

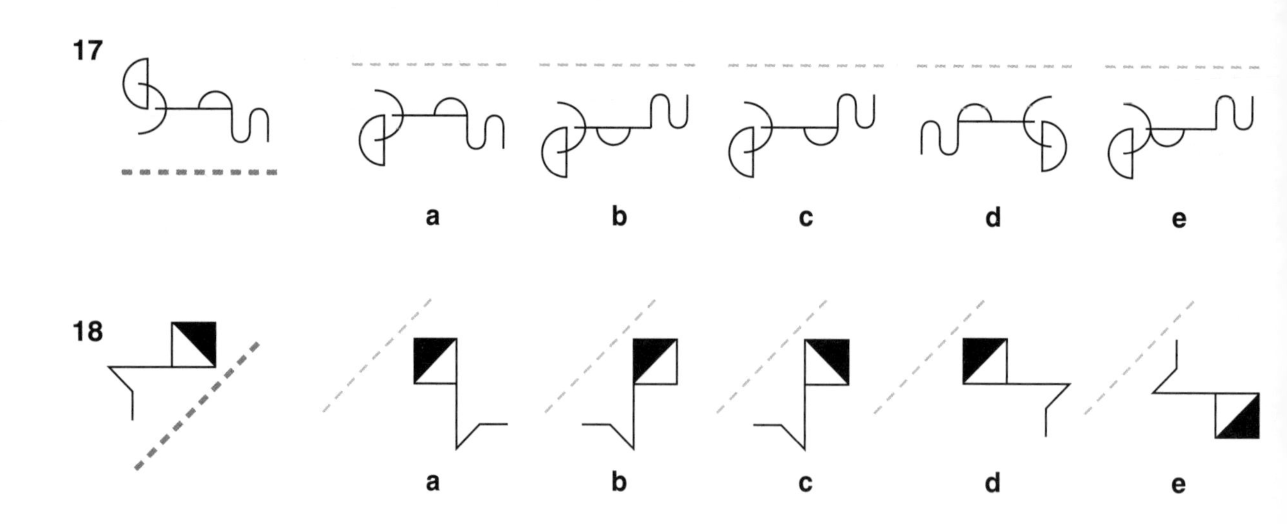

Which pattern on the right belongs in the group on the left? Circle the letter.

Example

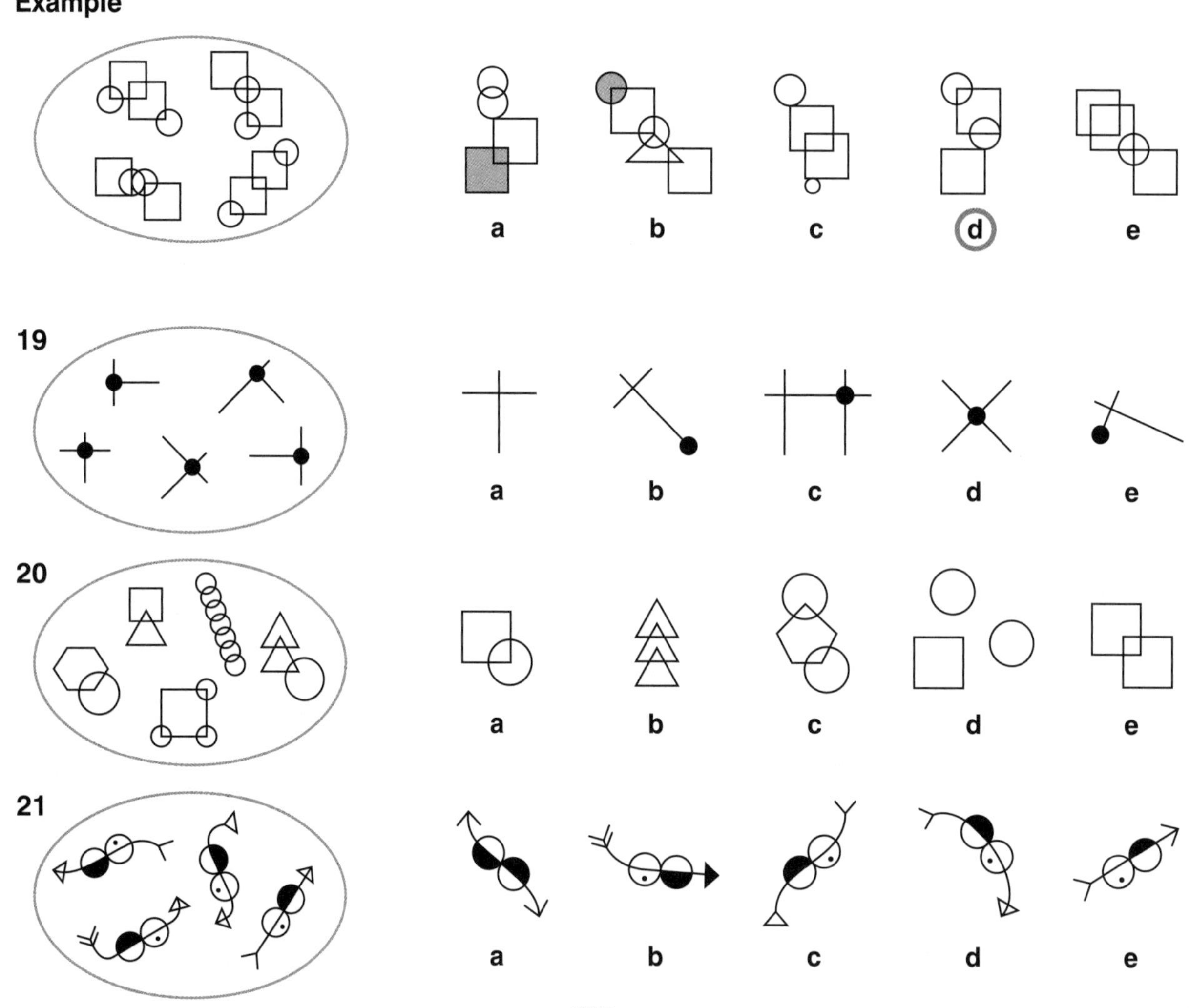

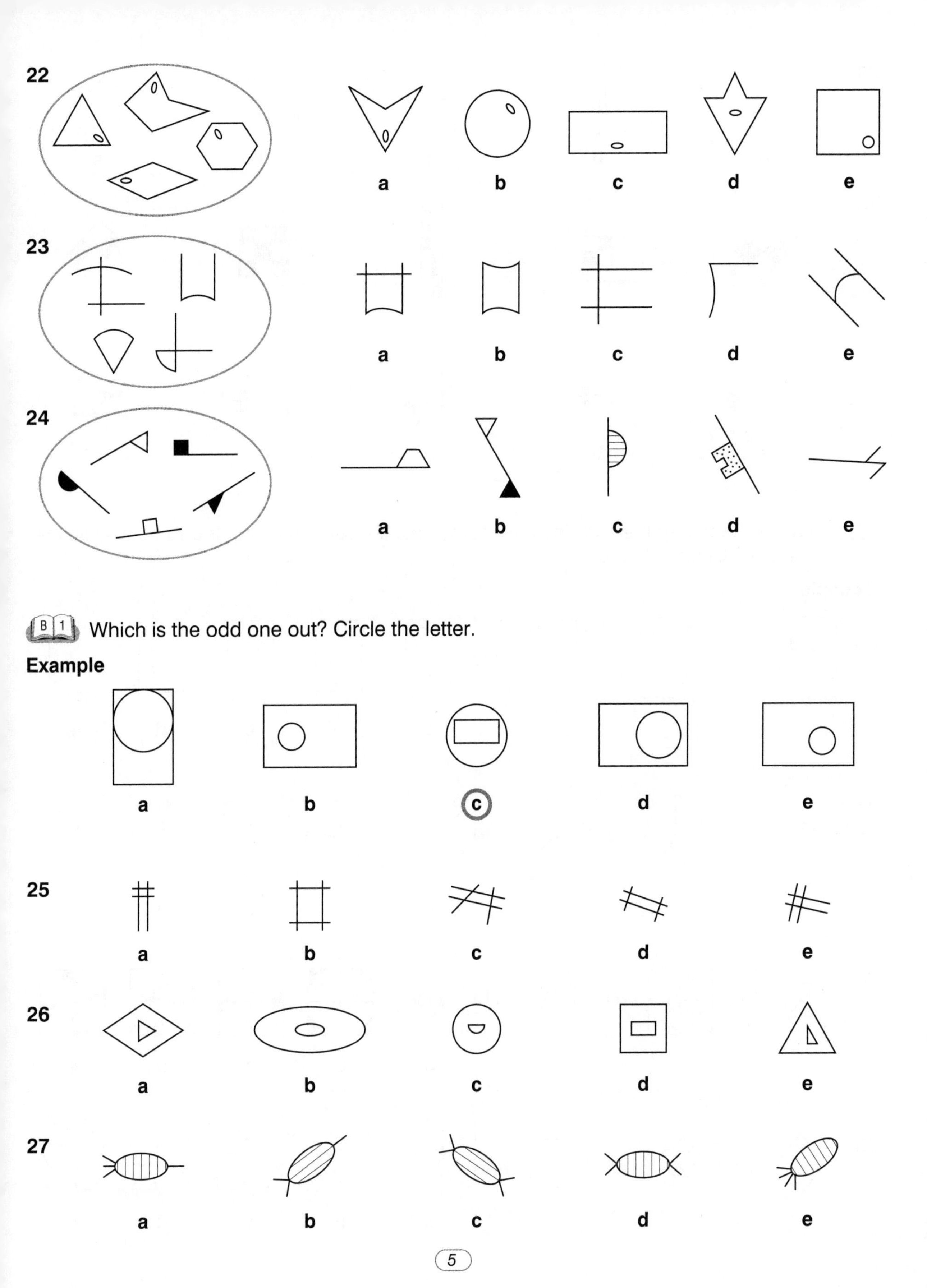
22
a
b
c
d
e
23
a
b
c
d
e
24
a
b
c
d
e
B 1
Which is the odd one out? Circle the letter.
Example
a
b
c
d
e
25
a
b
c
d
e
26
a
b
c
d
e
27
a
b
c
d
e
5

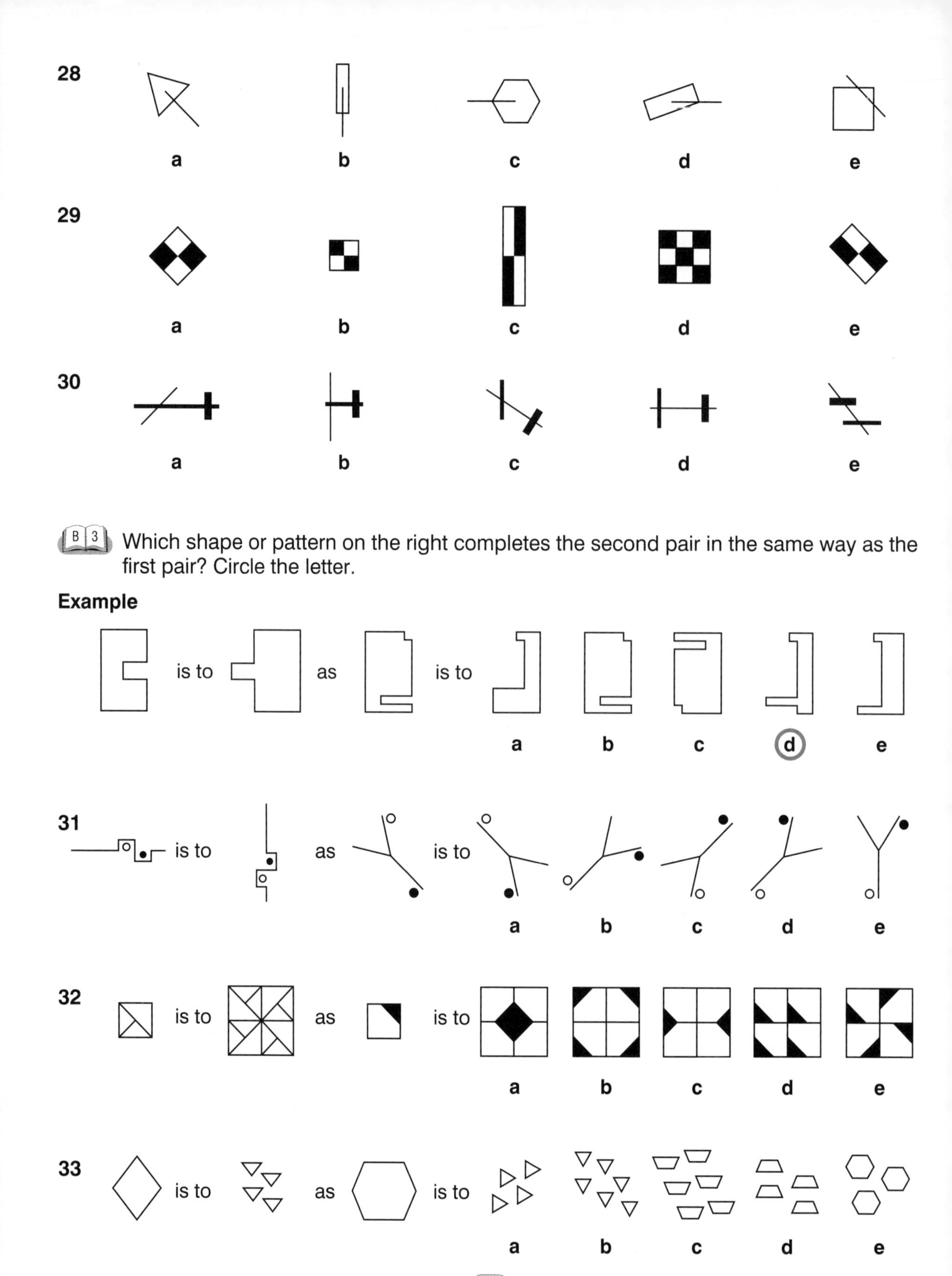

Which shape or pattern on the right completes the second pair in the same way as the first pair? Circle the letter.

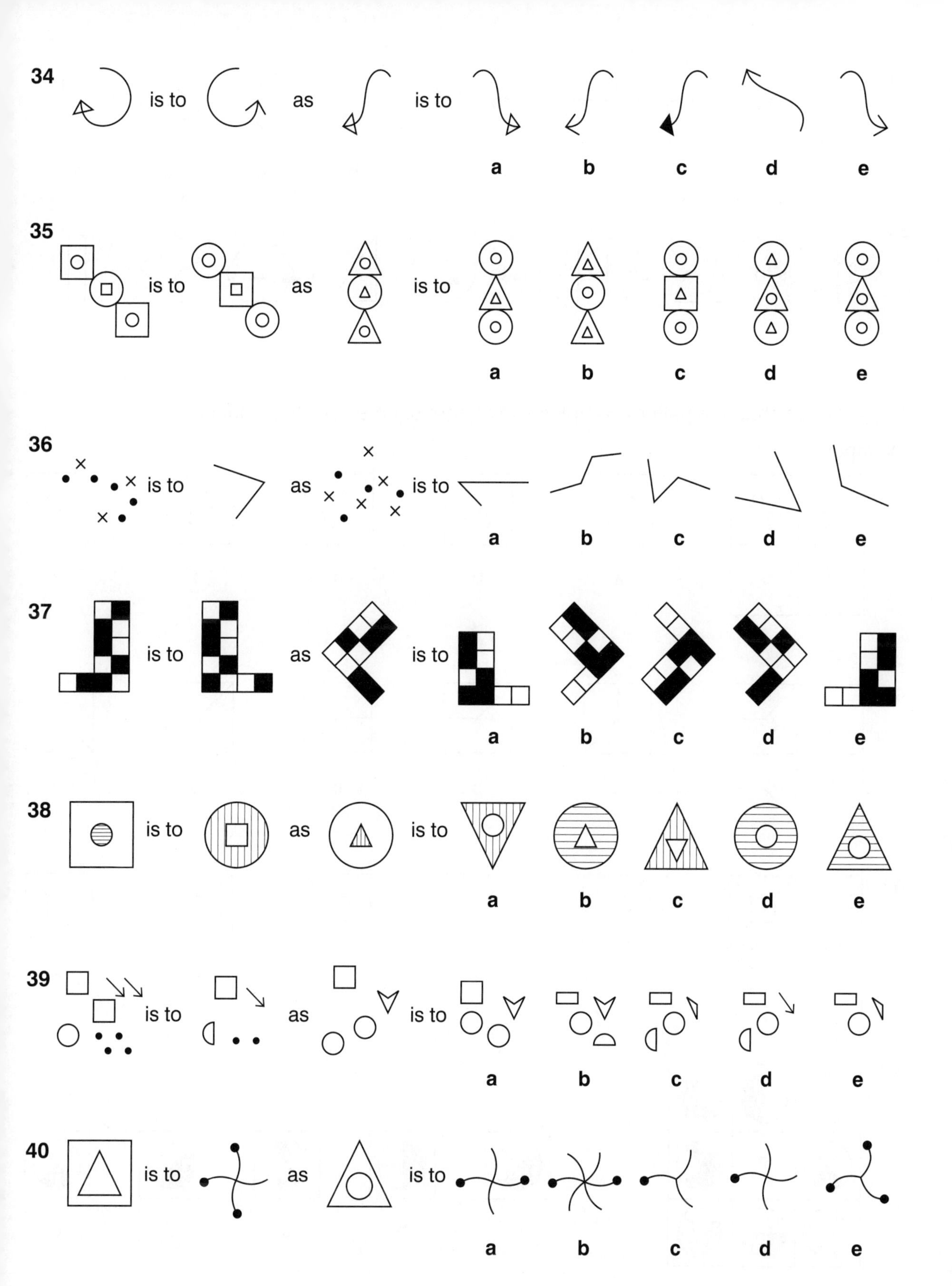
34
is to
as
is to
a
b
c
d
e
35
is to
as
is to
a
b
c
d
e
36
is to
as
is to
a
b
c
d
e
37
is to
as
is to
a
b
c
d
e
38
is to
as
is to
a
b
c
d
e
39
is to
as
is to
a
b
c
d
e
40
is to
as
is to
a
b
c
d
e

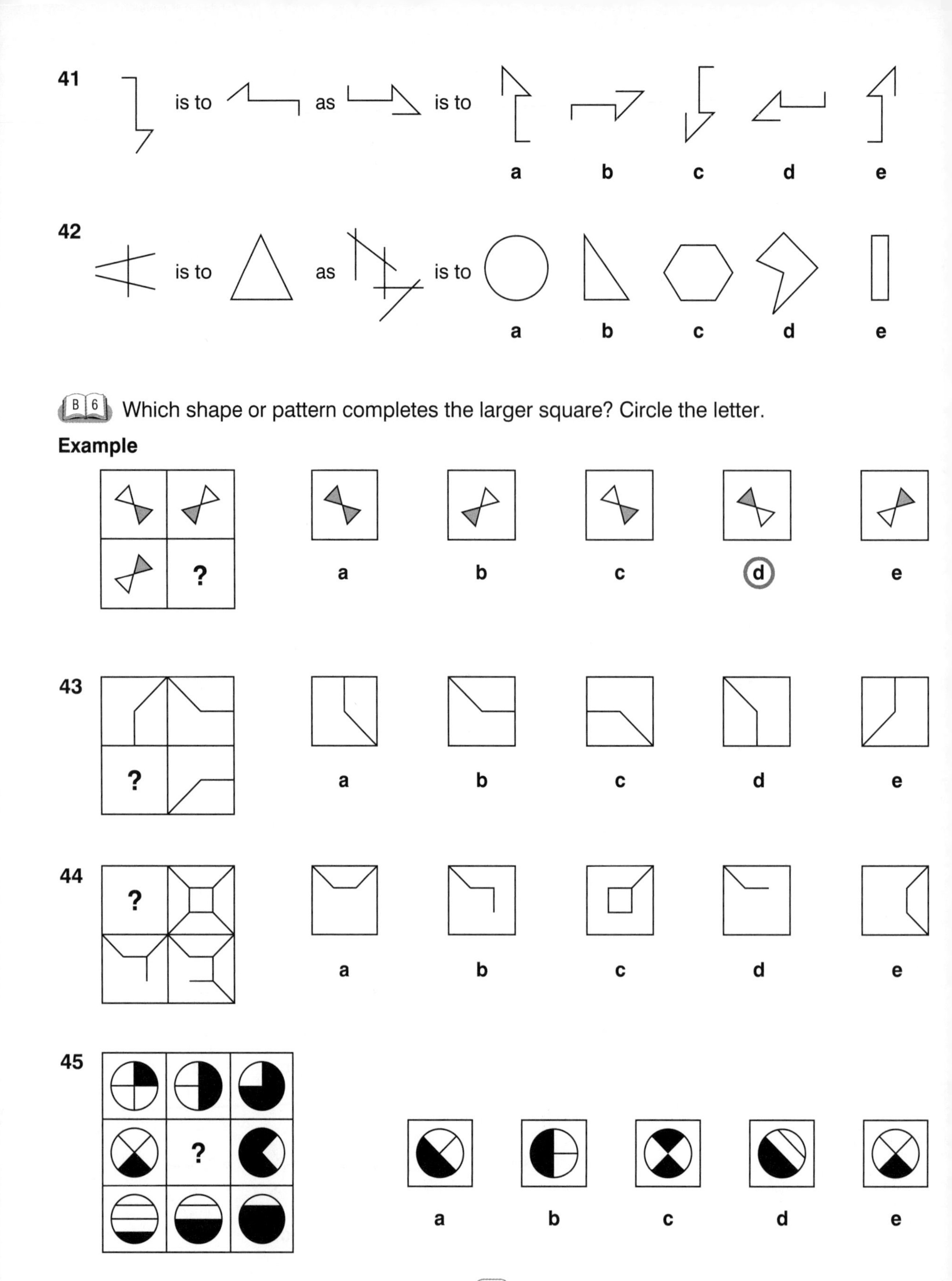
41
is to
as
is to
a
b
c
d
e
42
is to
as
is to
a
b
c
d
e
B 6
Which shape or pattern completes the larger square? Circle the letter.
Example
?
a
b
c
d
e
43
?
a
b
c
d
e
44
?
a
b
c
d
e
45
?
a
b
c
d
e

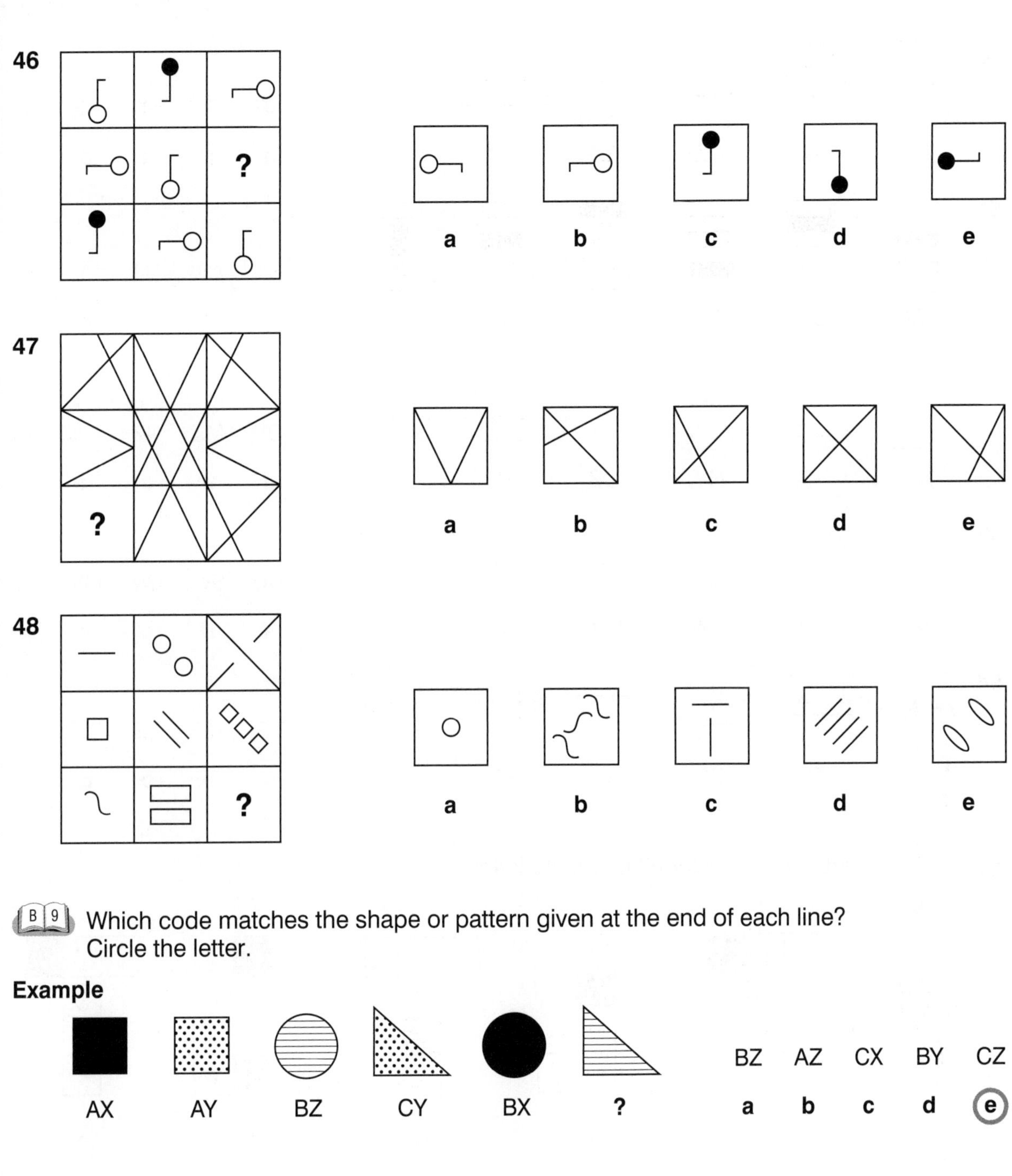

Which code matches the shape or pattern given at the end of each line?
Circle the letter.

Example

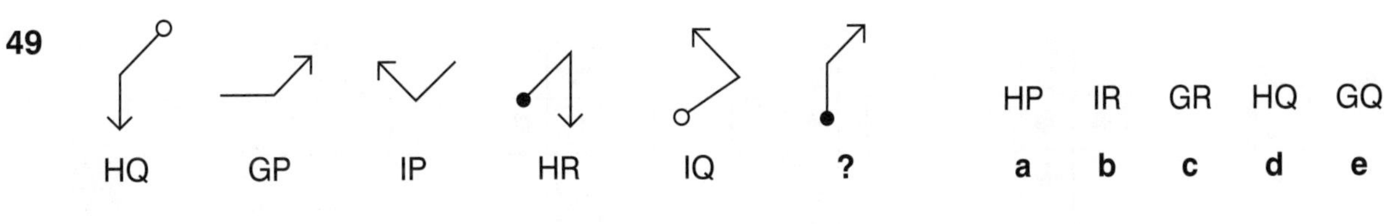

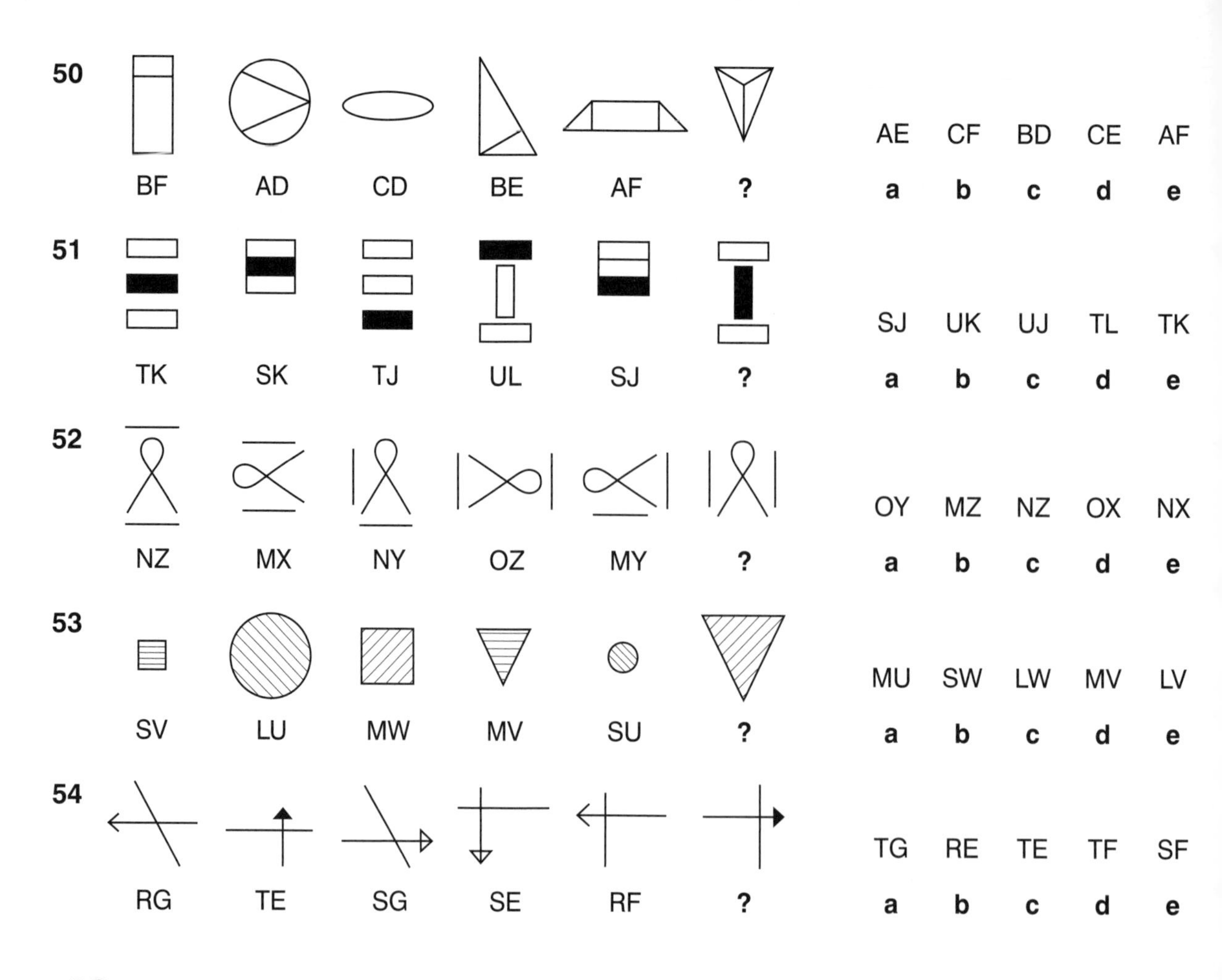

B8 Which net makes the cube? Circle the letter.

Example

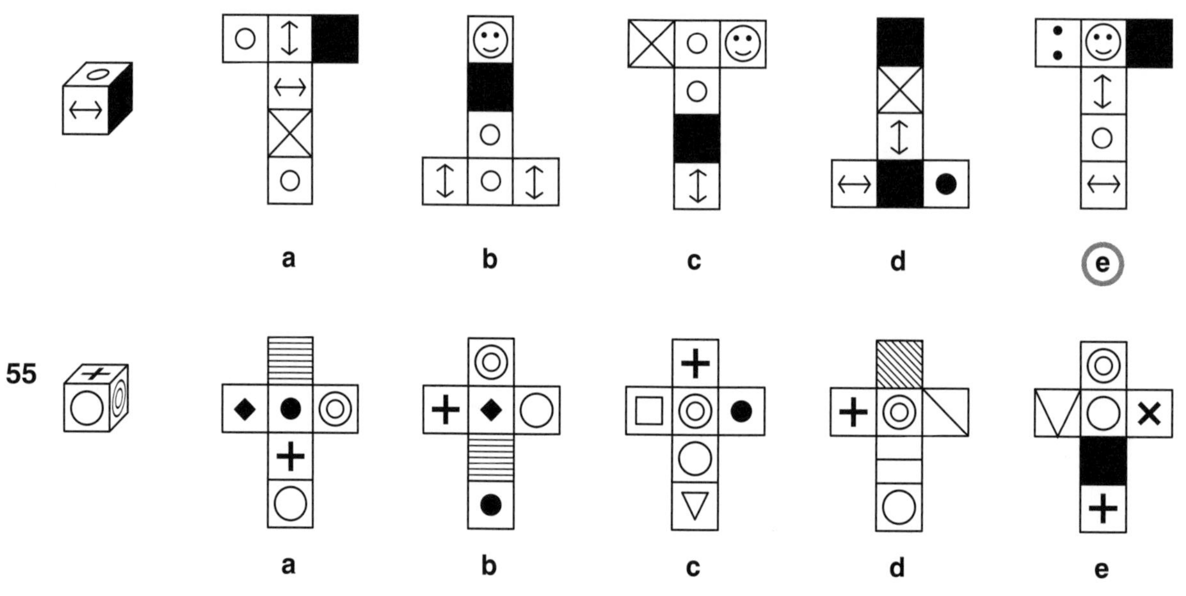

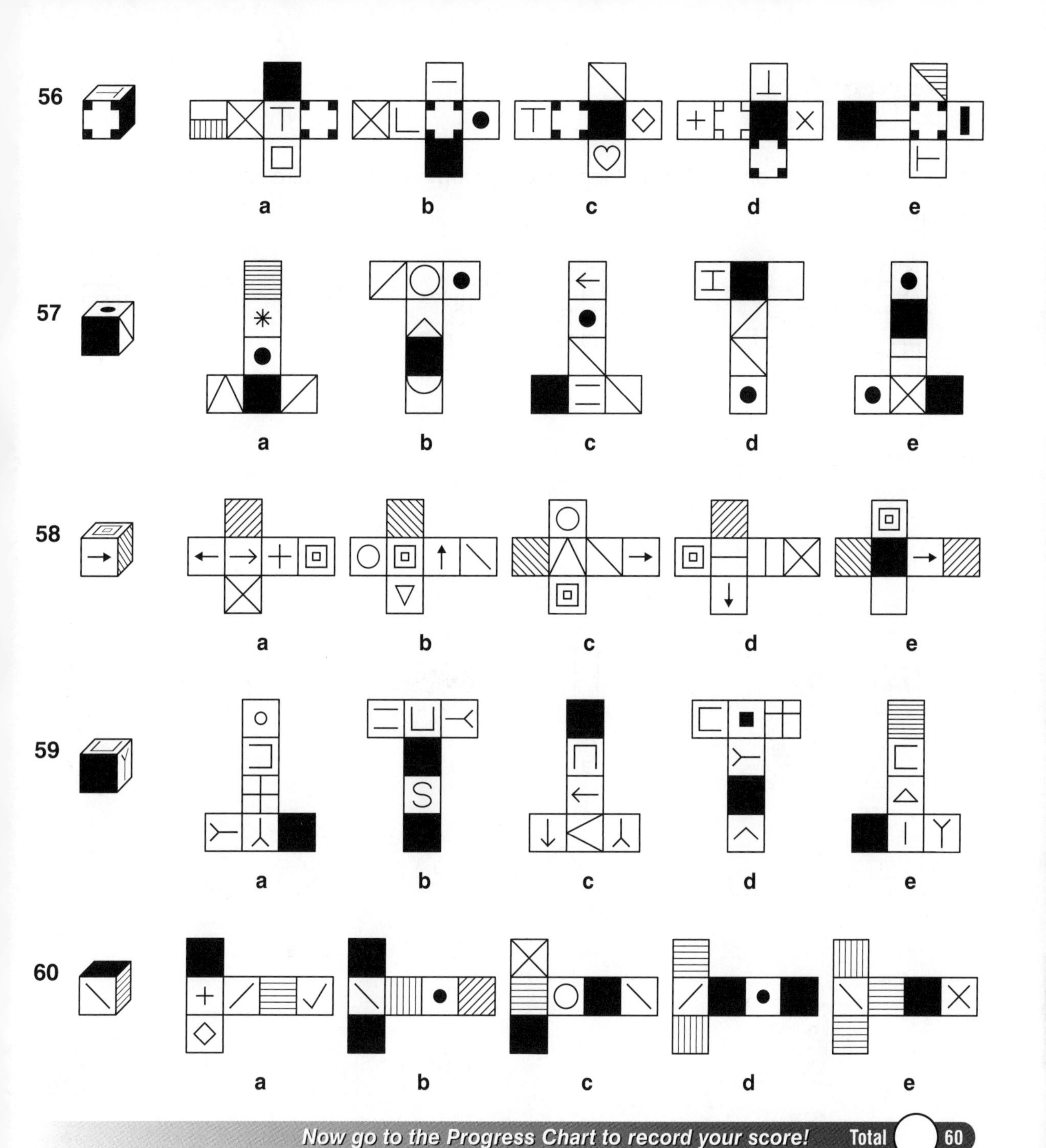

Now go to the Progress Chart to record your score! Total 60

Paper 2

B 2 Which pattern on the right belongs in the group on the left? Circle the letter.

Example

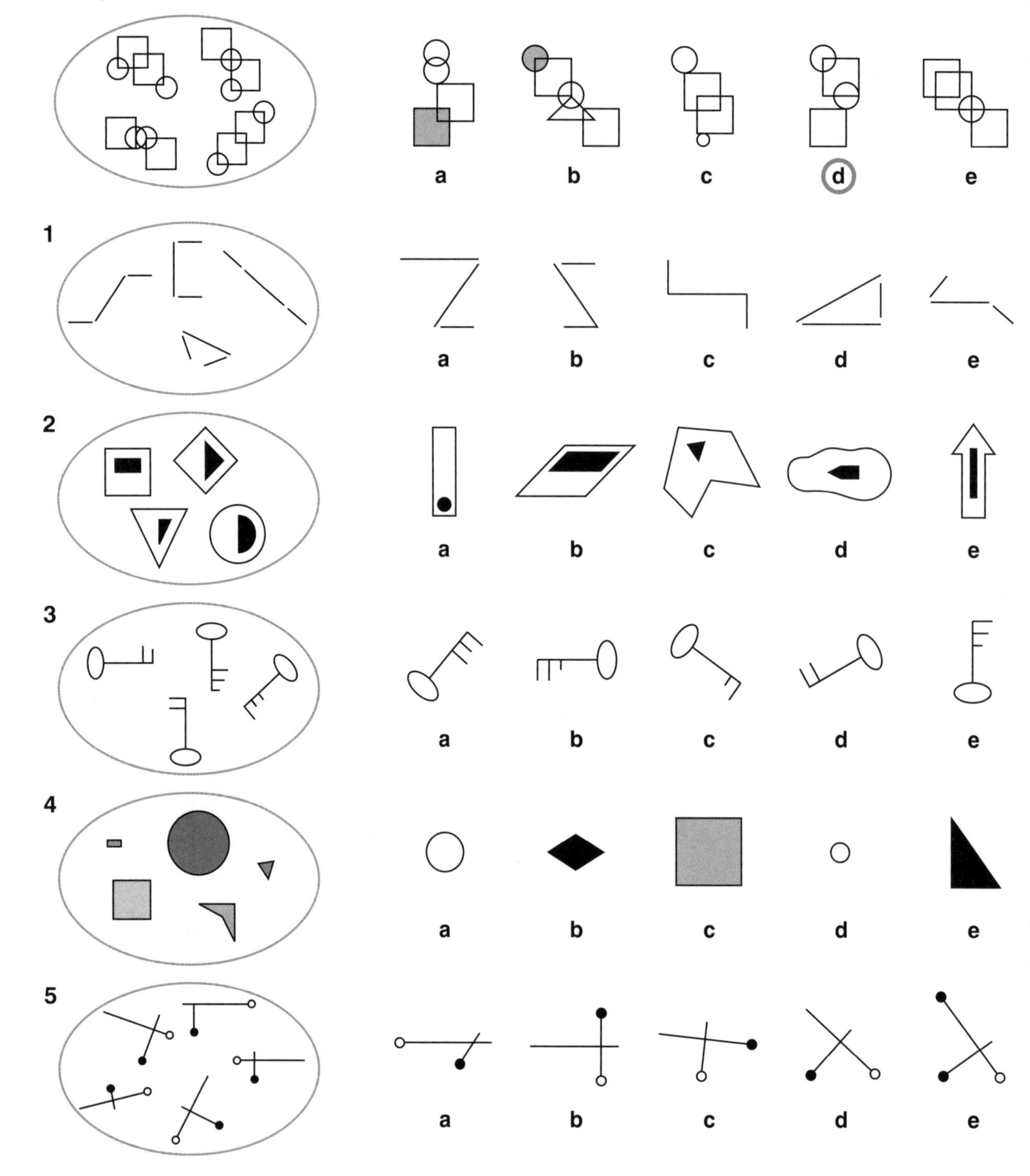

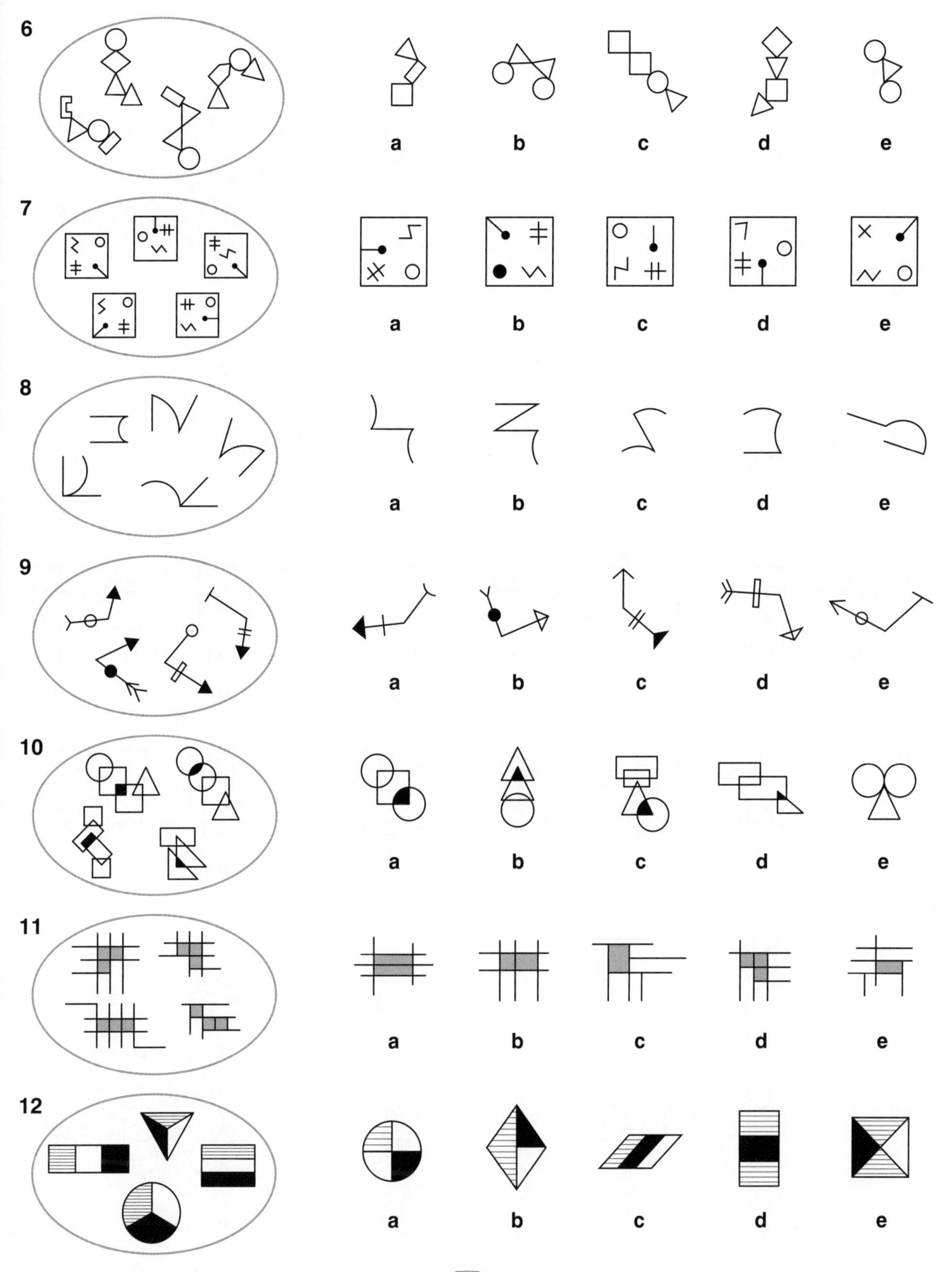
6
a
b
c
d
e
7
a
b
c
d
e
8
a
b
c
d
e
9
a
b
c
d
e
10
a
b
c
d
e
11
a
b
c
d
e
12
a
b
c
d
e

Which one comes next? Circle the letter.

Example

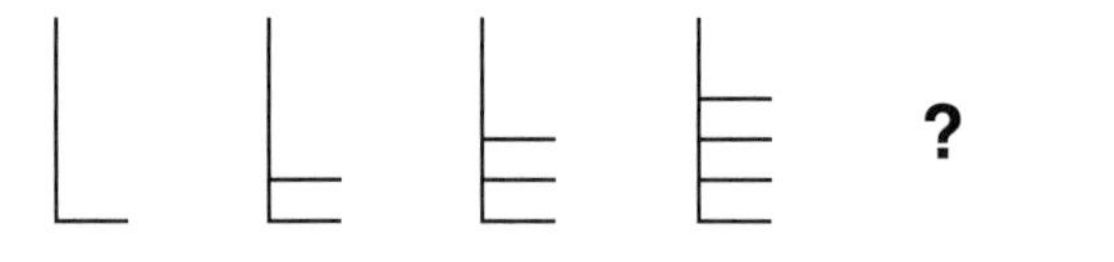

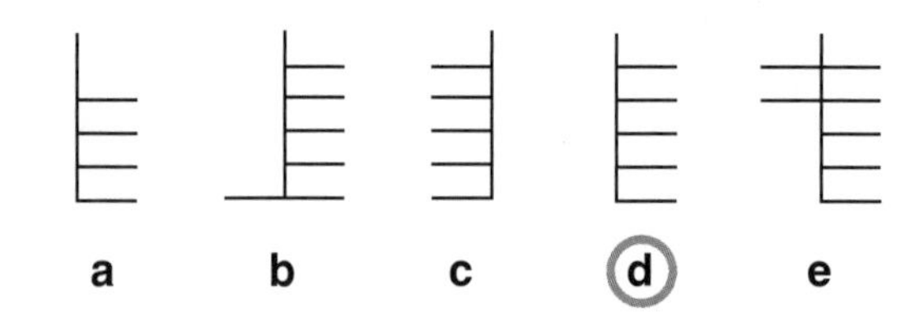

a b c (d) e

13

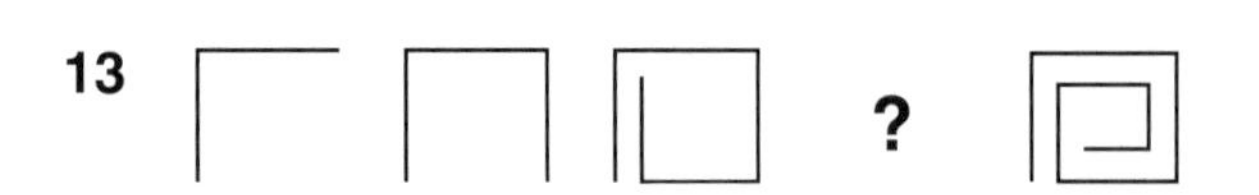

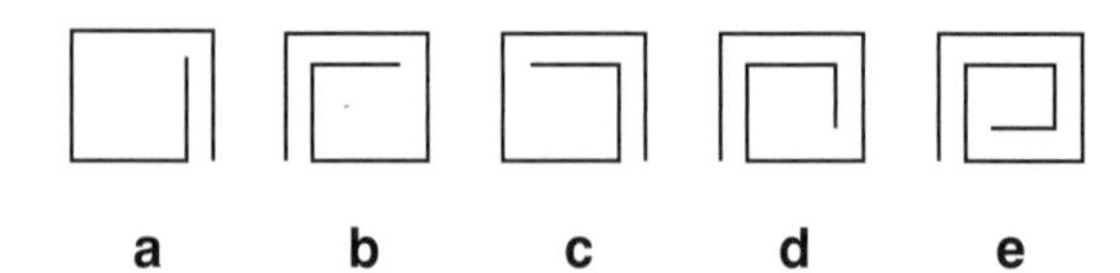

a b c d e

14

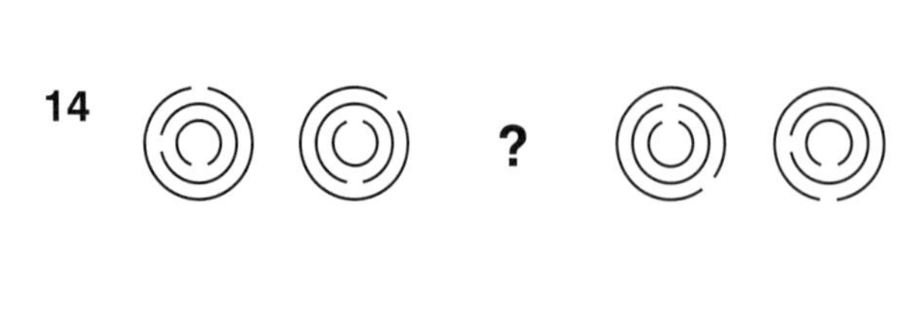

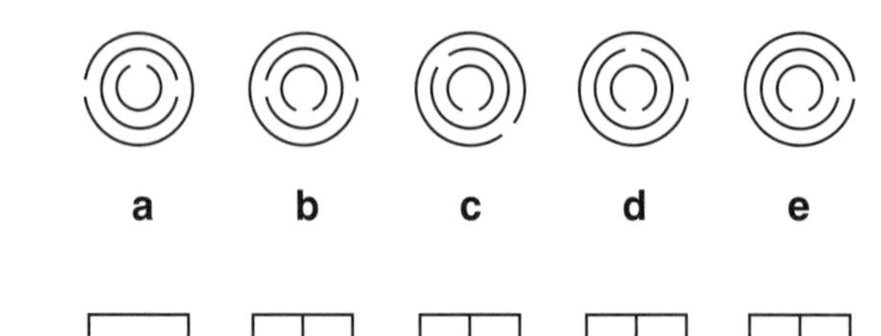

a b c d e

15

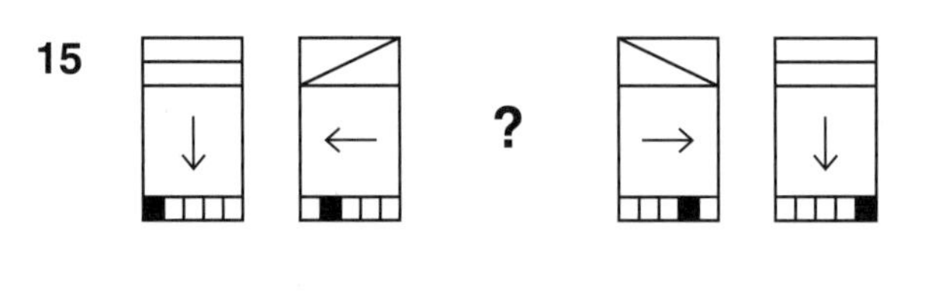

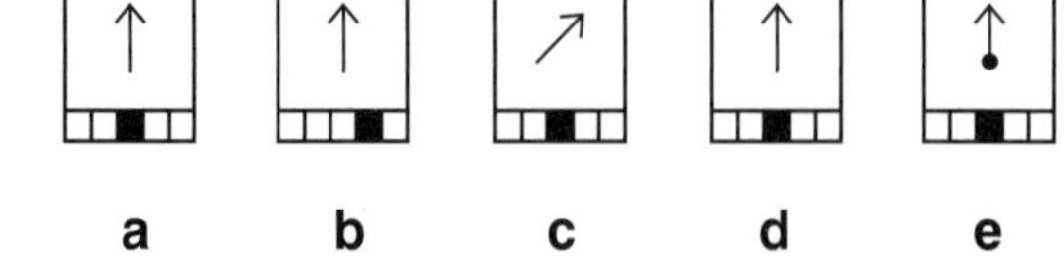

a b c d e

16

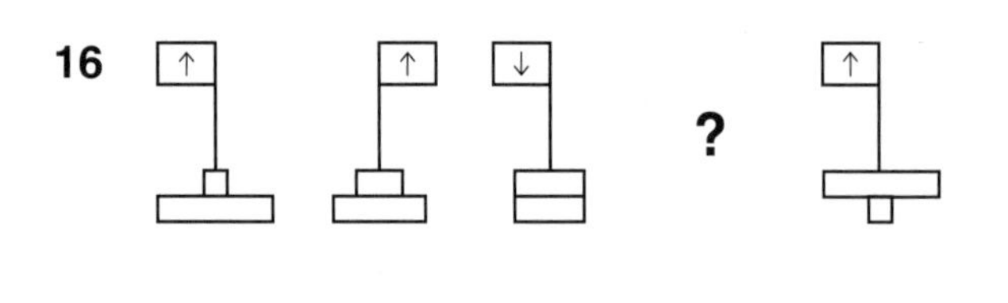

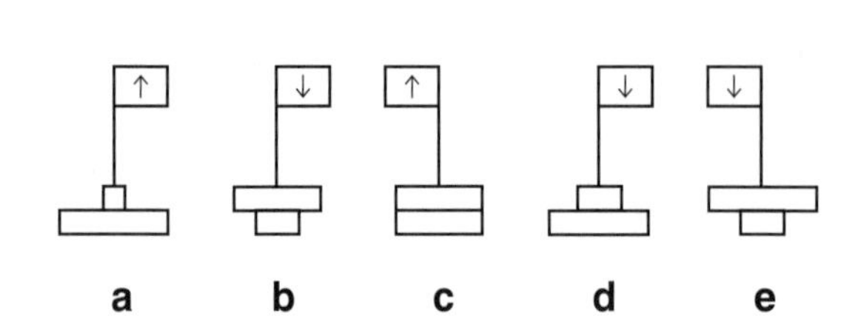

a b c d e

17

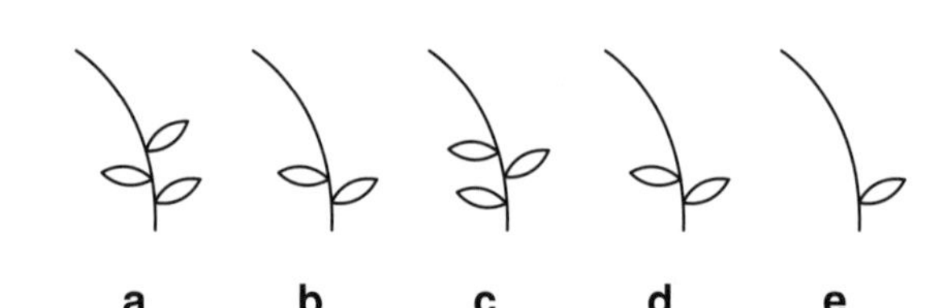

a b c d e

18

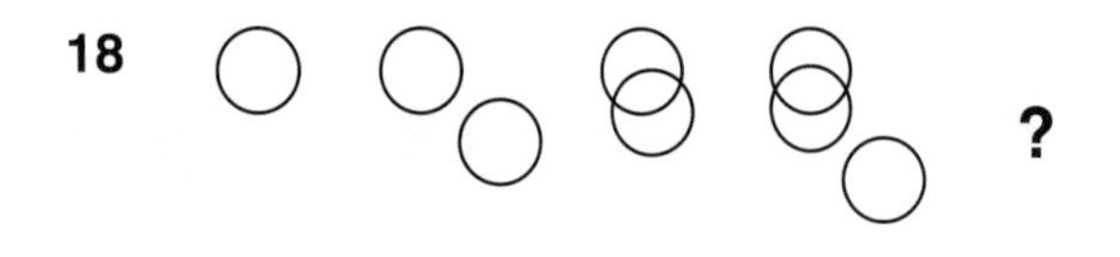

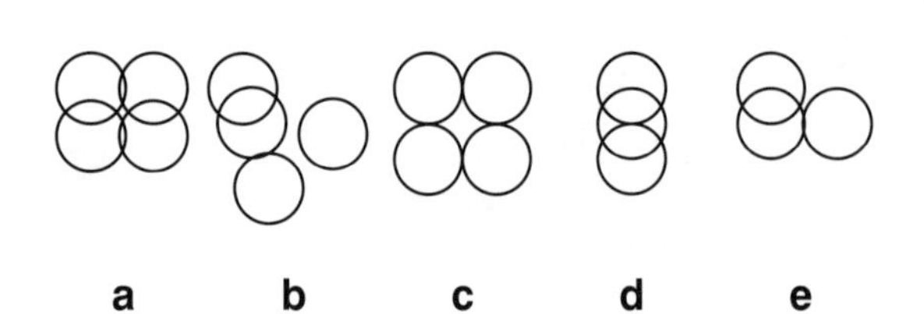

a b c d e

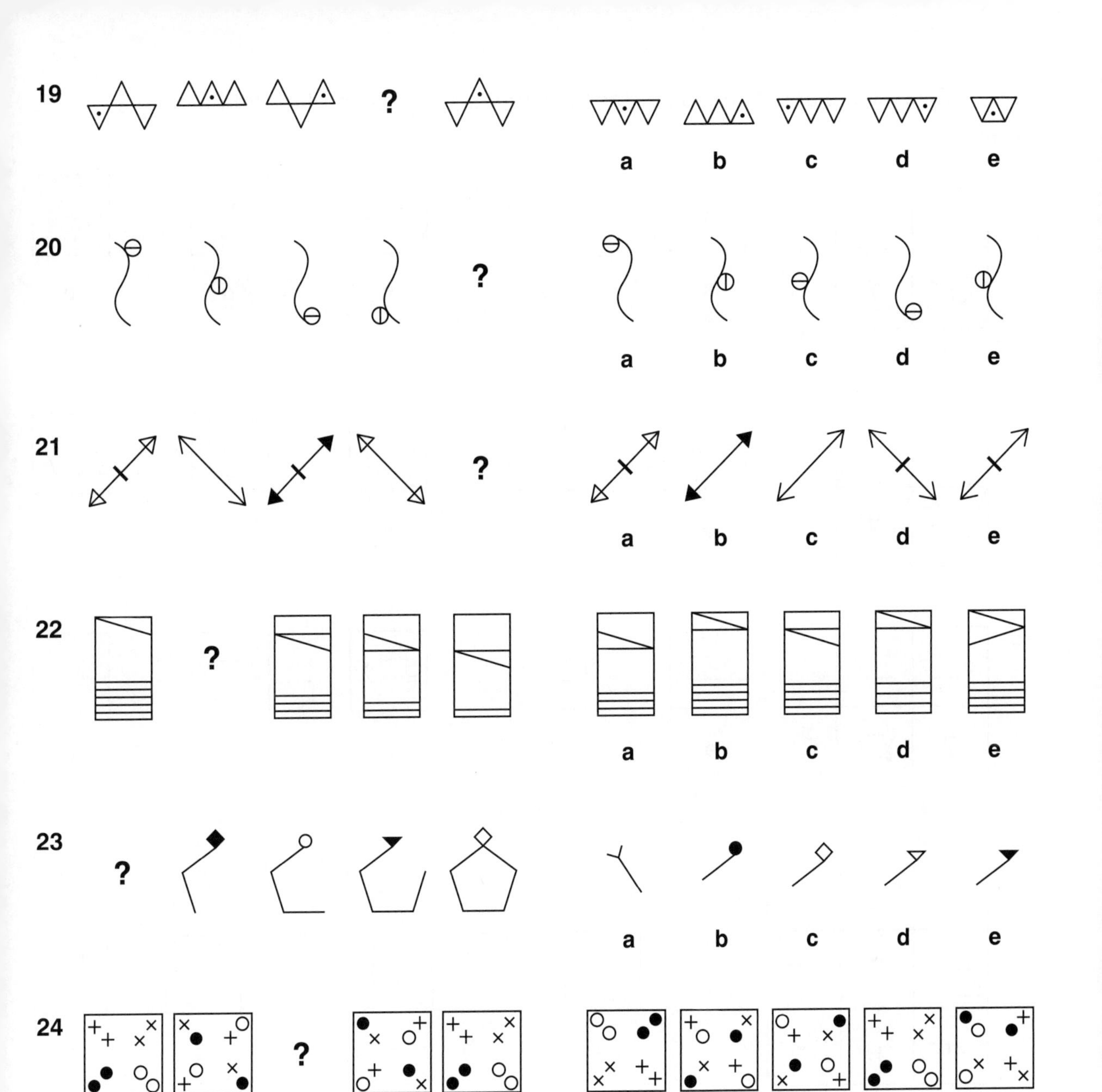
19
?
a b c d e
20
?
a b c d e
21
?
a b c d e
22
?
a b c d e
23
?
a b c d e
24
?
a b c d e

B6 Which shape or pattern completes the larger square? Circle the letter.

Example

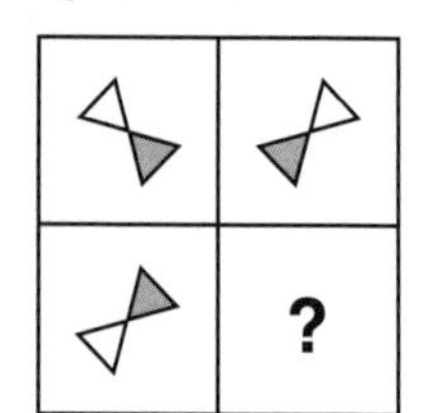

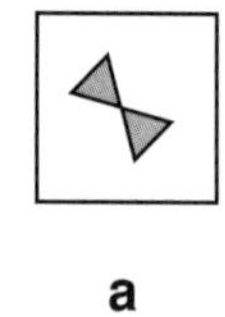

a

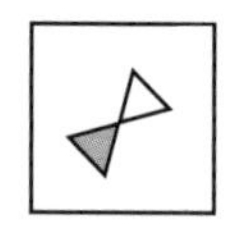

b

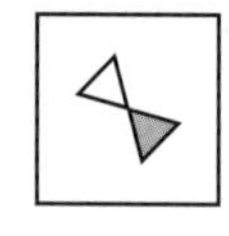

c

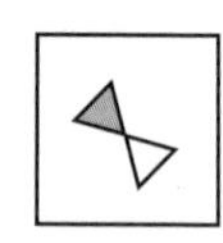

d

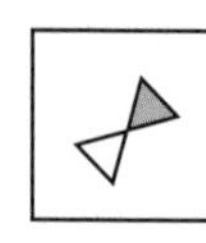

e

25

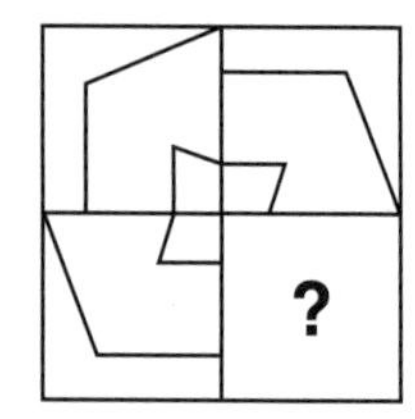

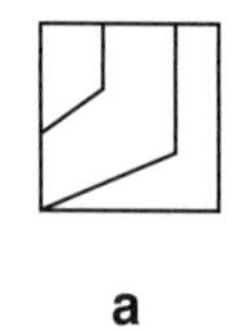

a b c d e

26

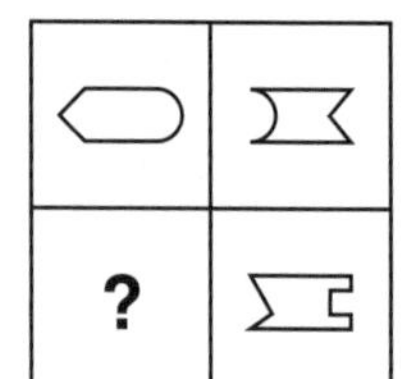

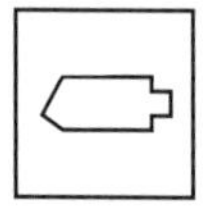

a b

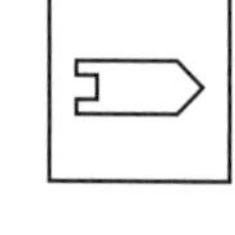

c d e

27

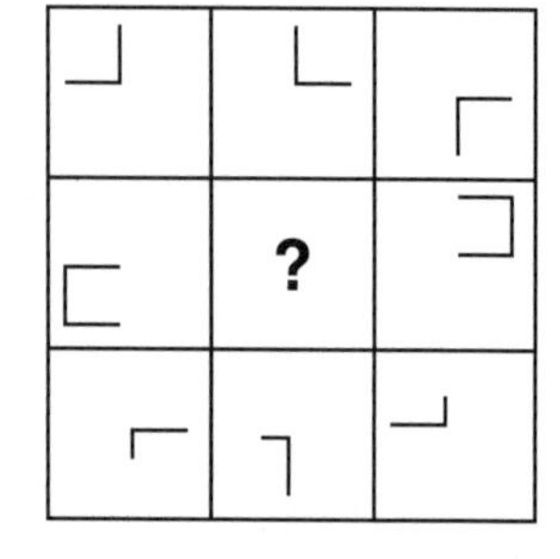

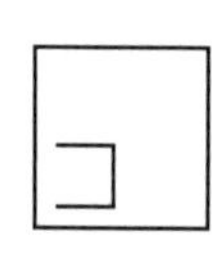

a

b

c

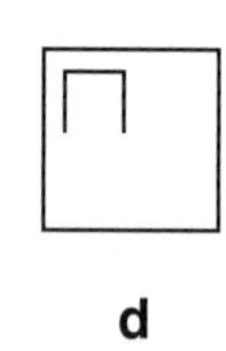

d e

28

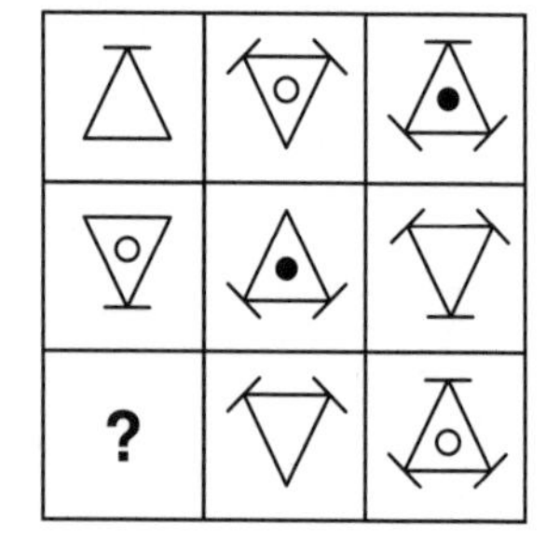

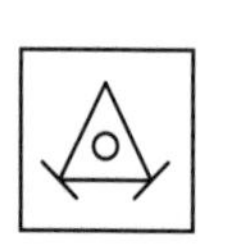

a

b

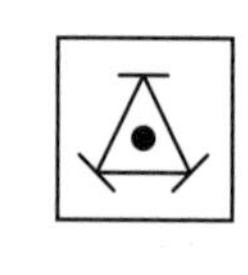

c

d

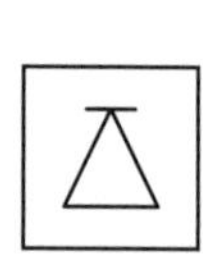

e

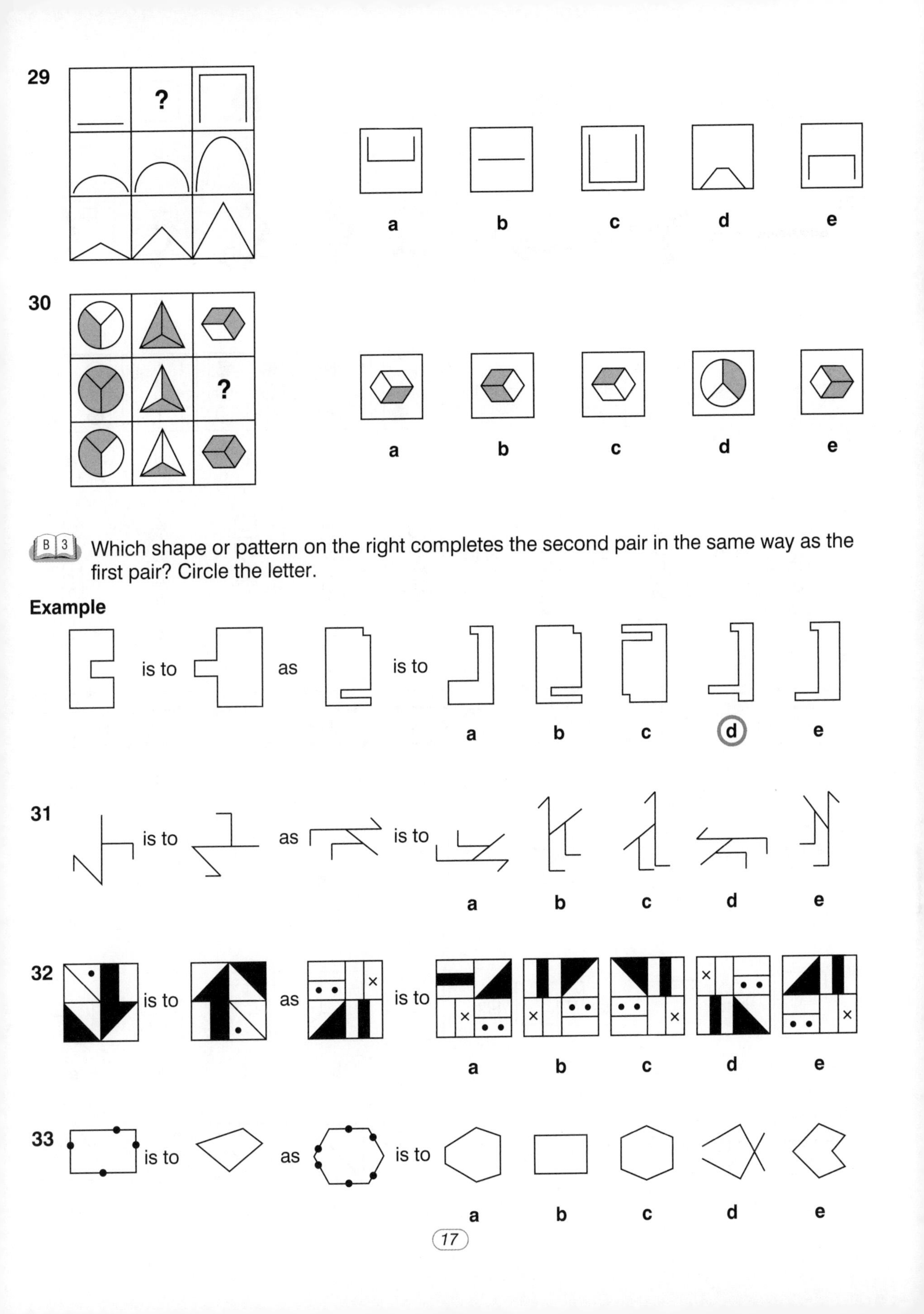
29
?
a
b
c
d
e
30
?
a
b
c
d
e
B 3
Which shape or pattern on the right completes the second pair in the same way as the first pair? Circle the letter.
Example
is to
as
is to
a
b
c
d
e
31
is to
as
is to
a
b
c
d
e
32
is to
as
is to
a
b
c
d
e
33
is to
as
is to
a
b
c
d
e
17

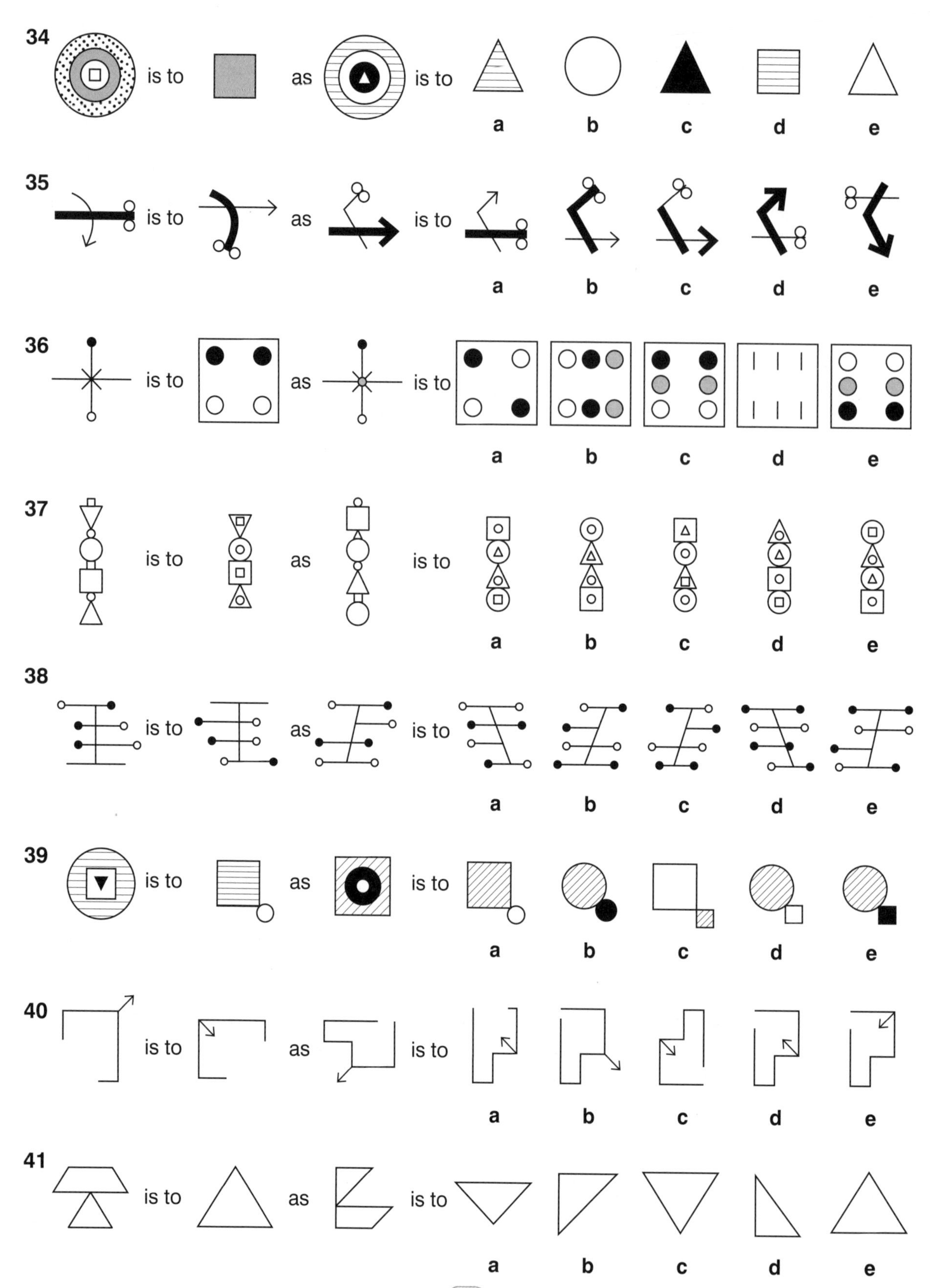
34
is to
as
is to
a
b
c
d
e
35
is to
as
is to
a
b
c
d
e
36
is to
as
is to
a
b
c
d
e
37
is to
as
is to
a
b
c
d
e
38
is to
as
is to
a
b
c
d
e
39
is to
as
is to
a
b
c
d
e
40
is to
as
is to
a
b
c
d
e
41
is to
as
is to
a
b
c
d
e

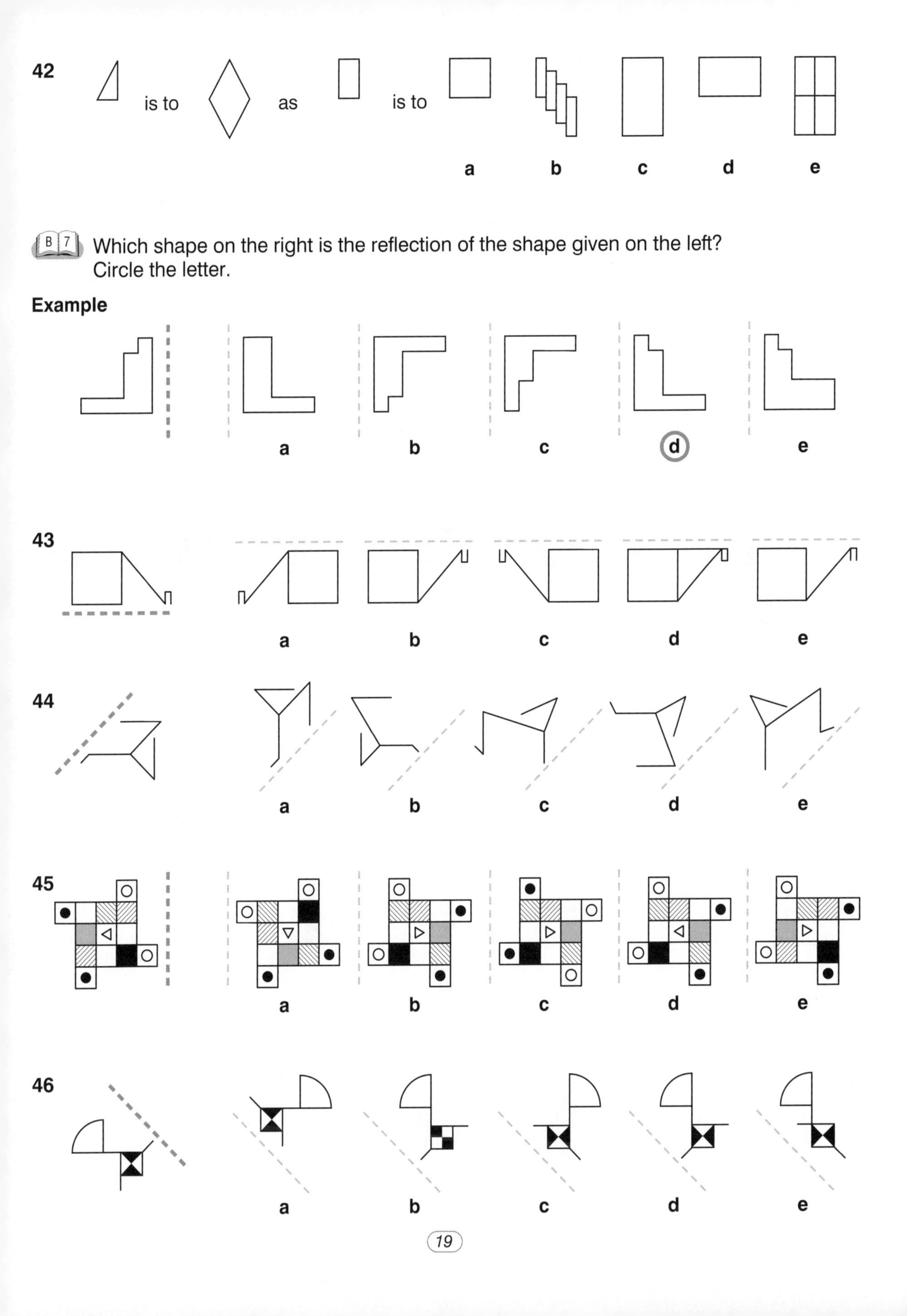
42
is to
as
is to
a
b
c
d
e
Which shape on the right is the reflection of the shape given on the left?
Circle the letter.
Example
a
b
c
d
e
43
a
b
c
d
e
44
a
b
c
d
e
45
a
b
c
d
e
46
a
b
c
d
e

47

48

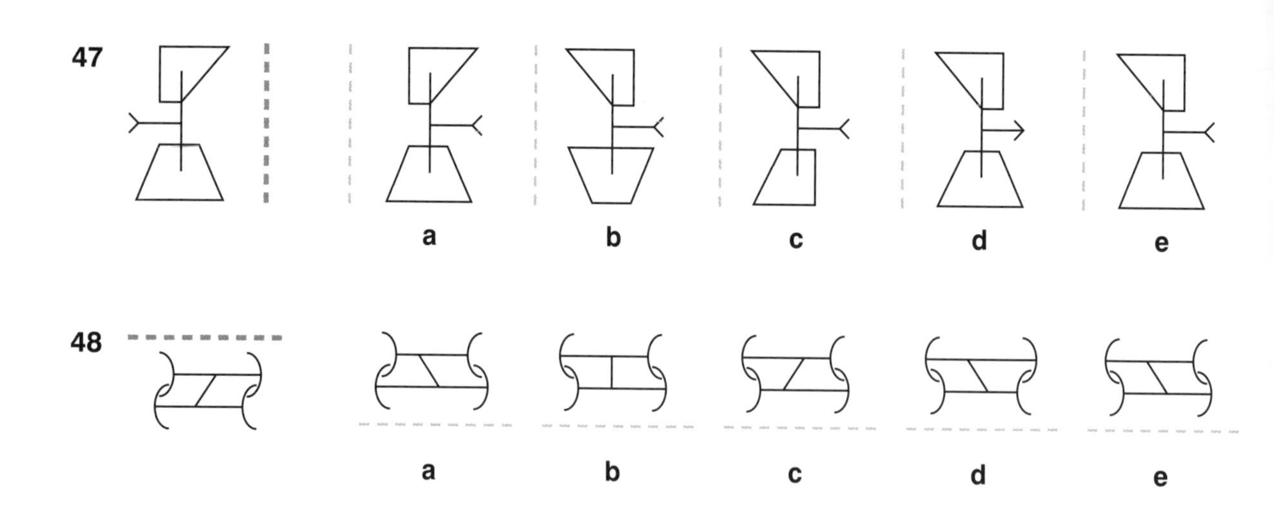

B8 Which cube cannot be made from the given net? Circle the letter.

Example

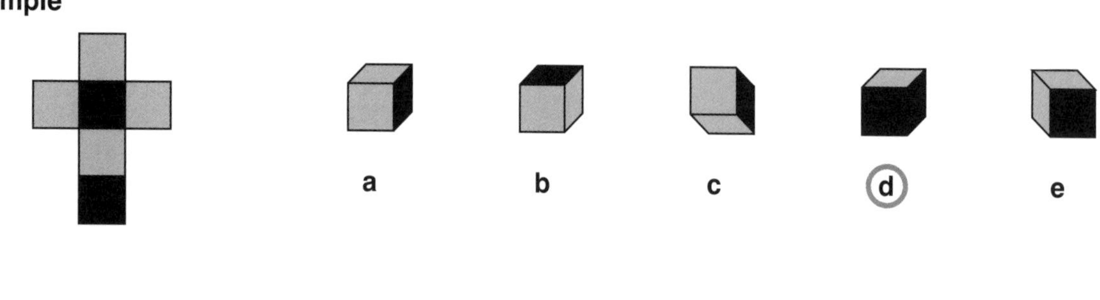

49

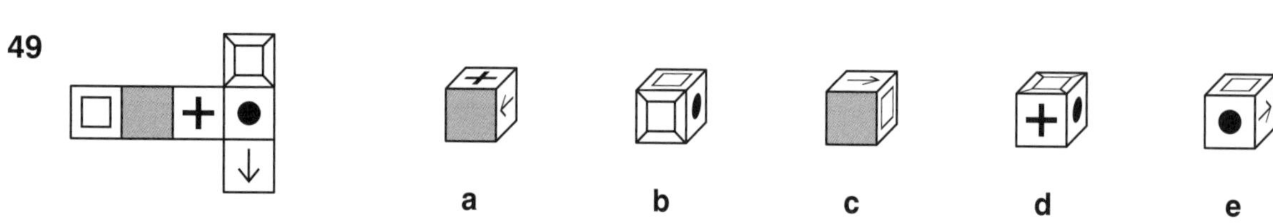

50

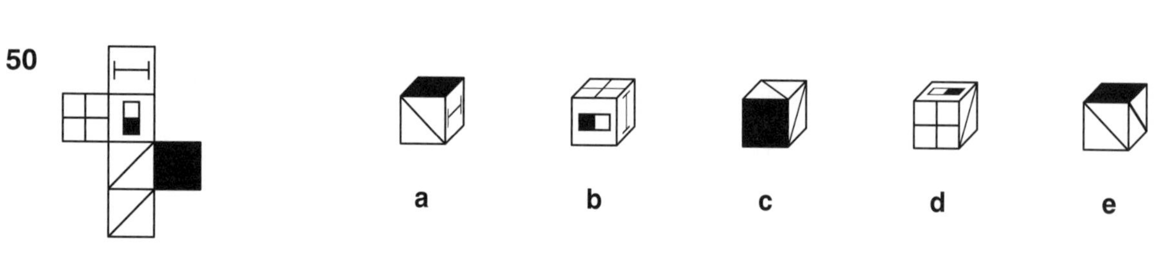

51

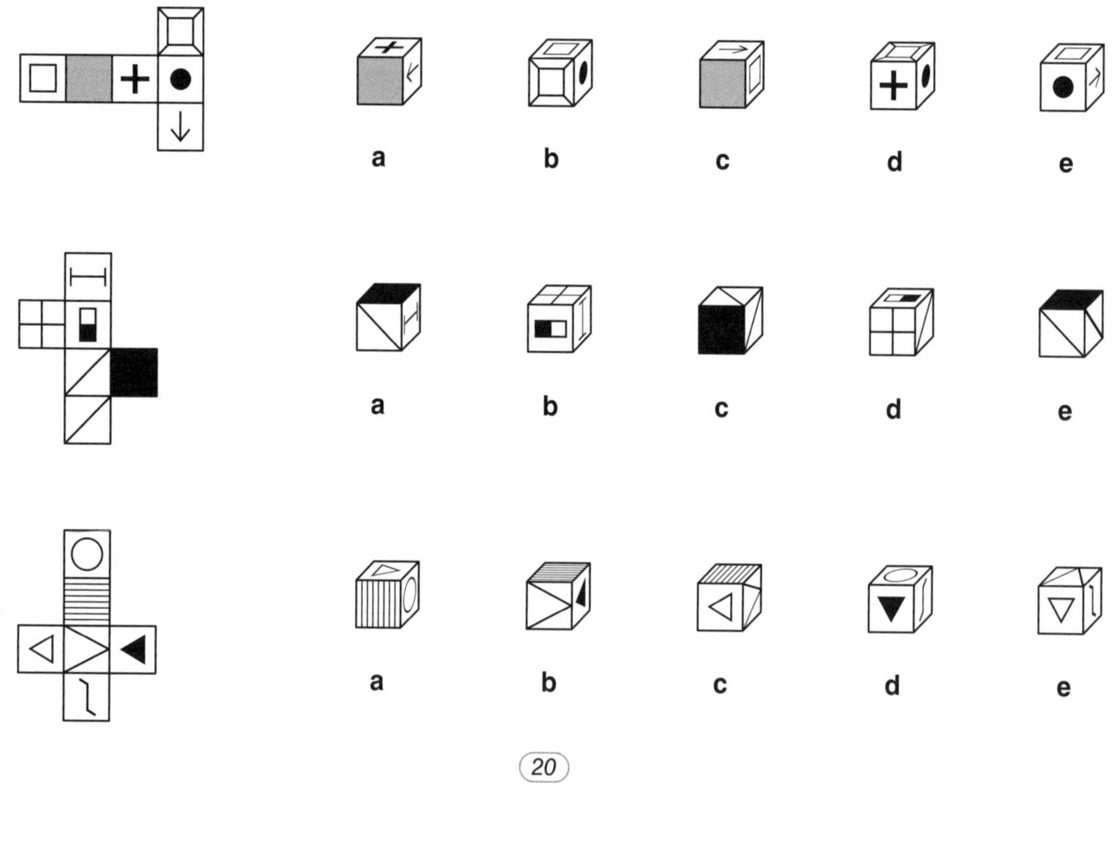

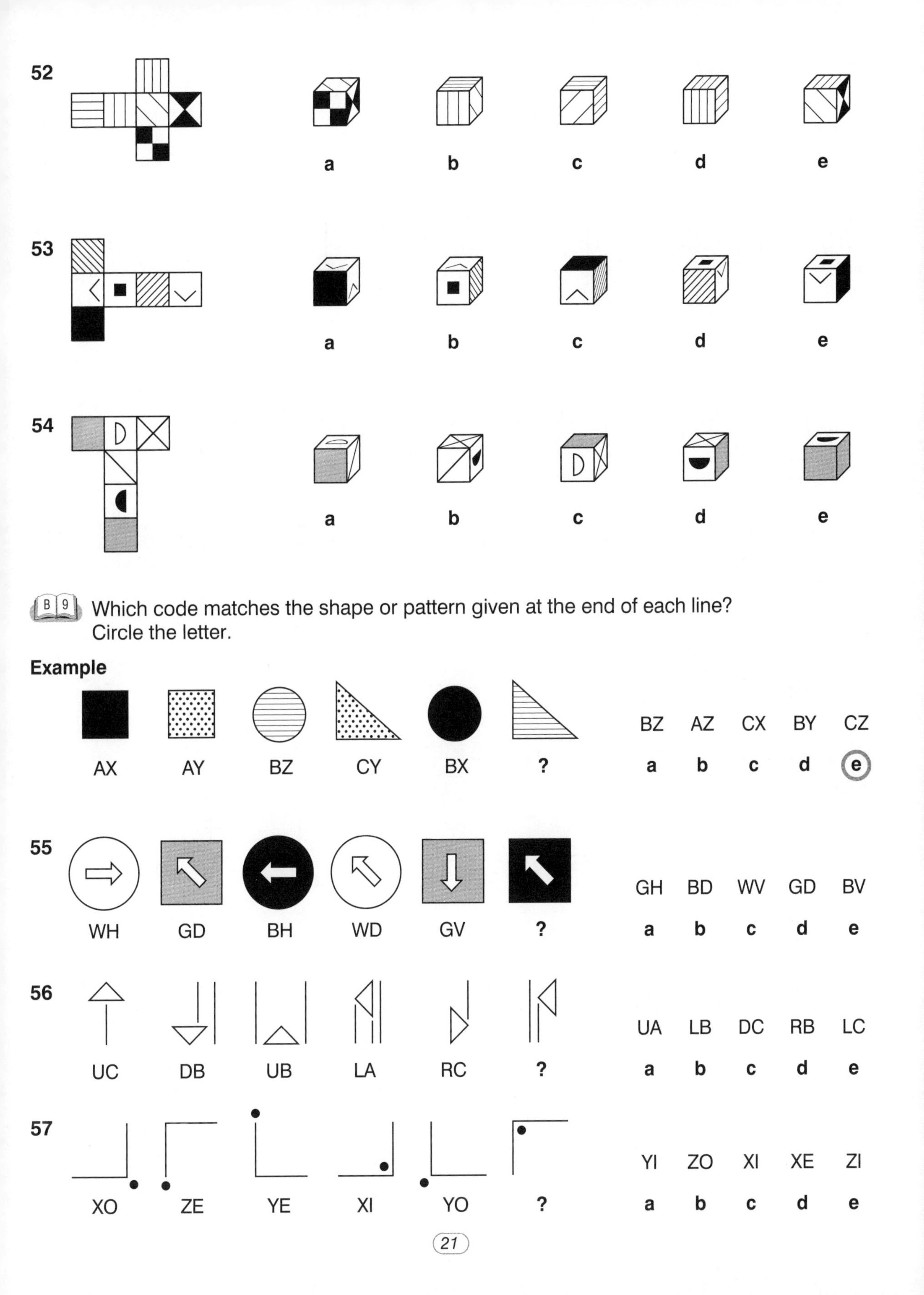
52
a
b
c
d
e
53
a
b
c
d
e
54
a
b
c
d
e
B 9
Which code matches the shape or pattern given at the end of each line?
Circle the letter.
Example
AX
AY
BZ
CY
BX
?
BZ AZ CX BY CZ
a b c d e
55
WH
GD
BH
WD
GV
?
GH BD WV GD BV
a b c d e
56
UC
DB
UB
LA
RC
?
UA LB DC RB LC
a b c d e
57
XO
ZE
YE
XI
YO
?
YI ZO XI XE ZI
a b c d e
21

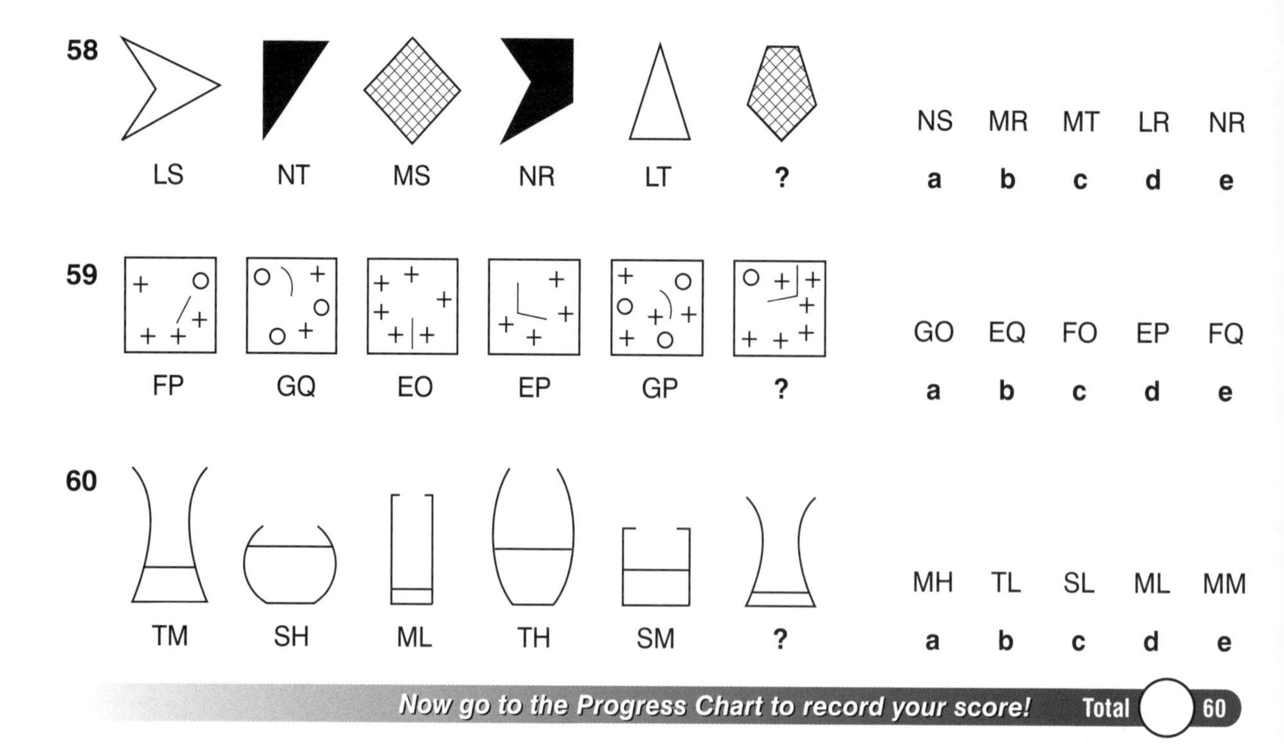

Now go to the Progress Chart to record your score! Total 60

Paper 3

B 4 Which one comes next? Circle the letter.

Example

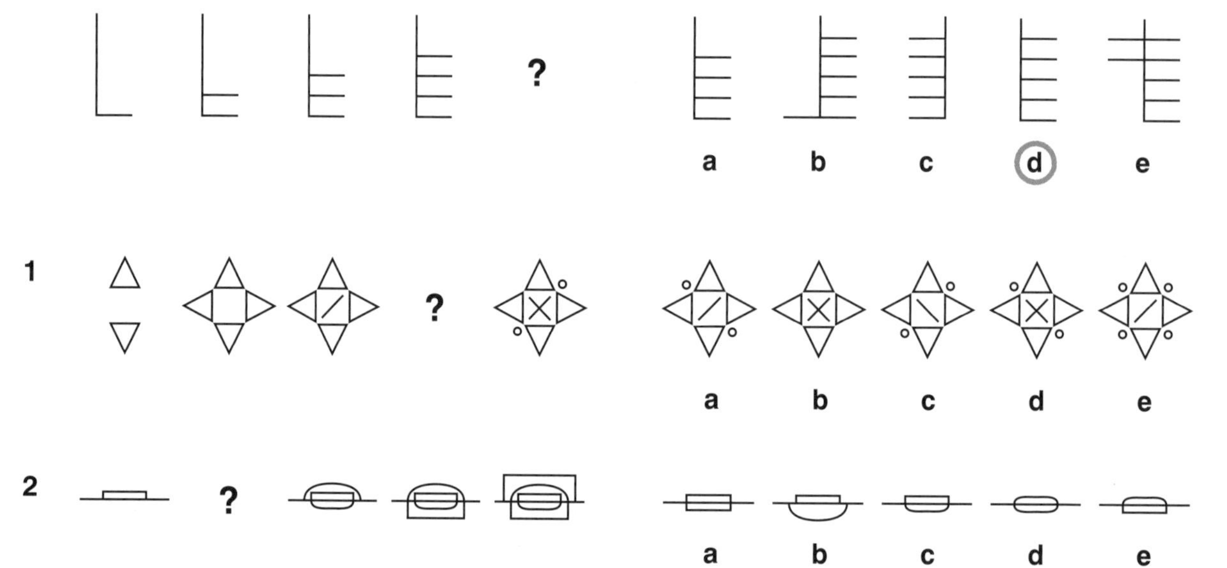

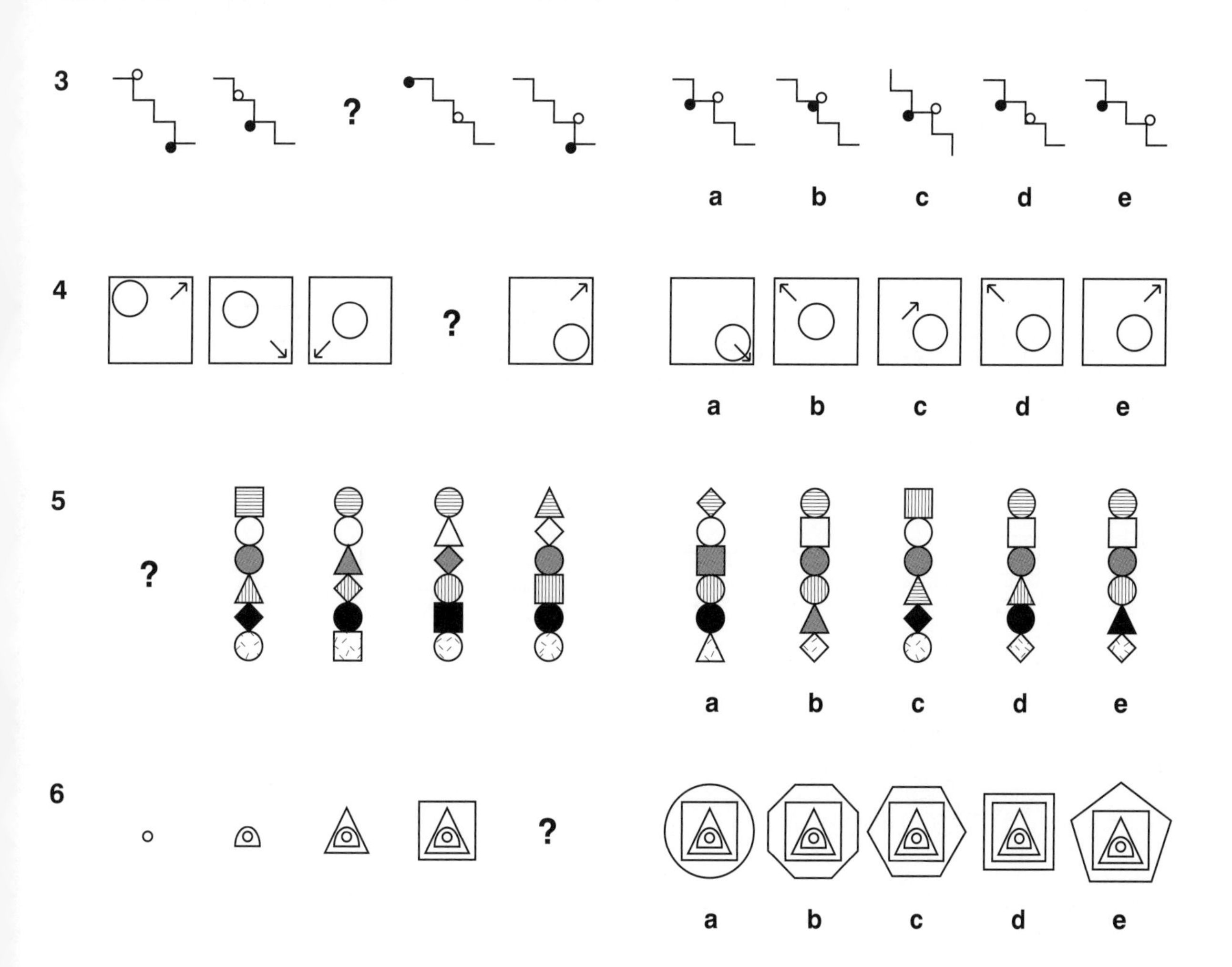

B 2 Which pattern on the right belongs in the group on the left? Circle the letter.

Example

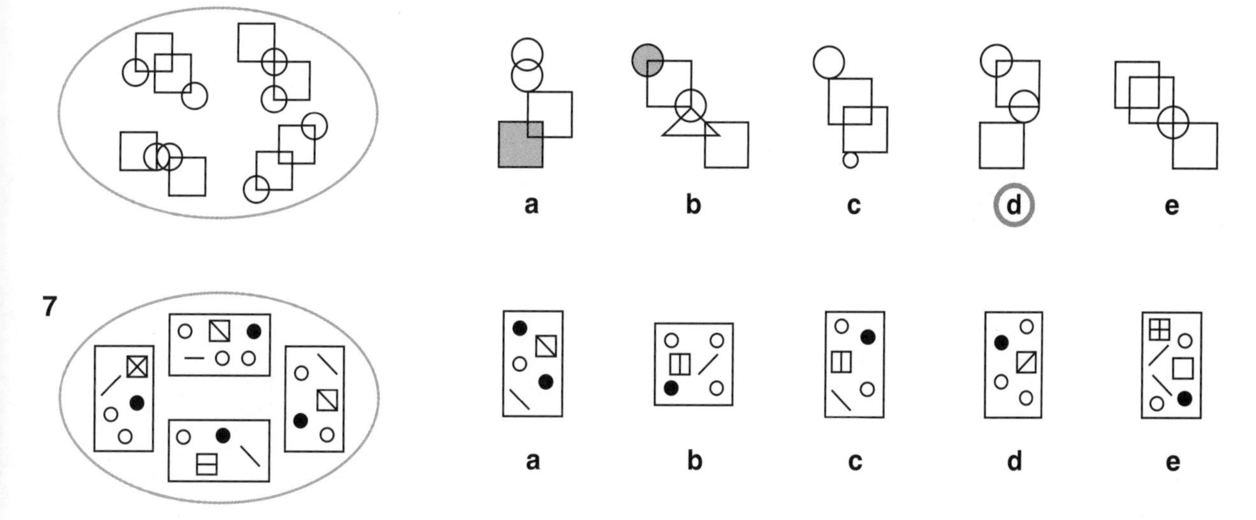

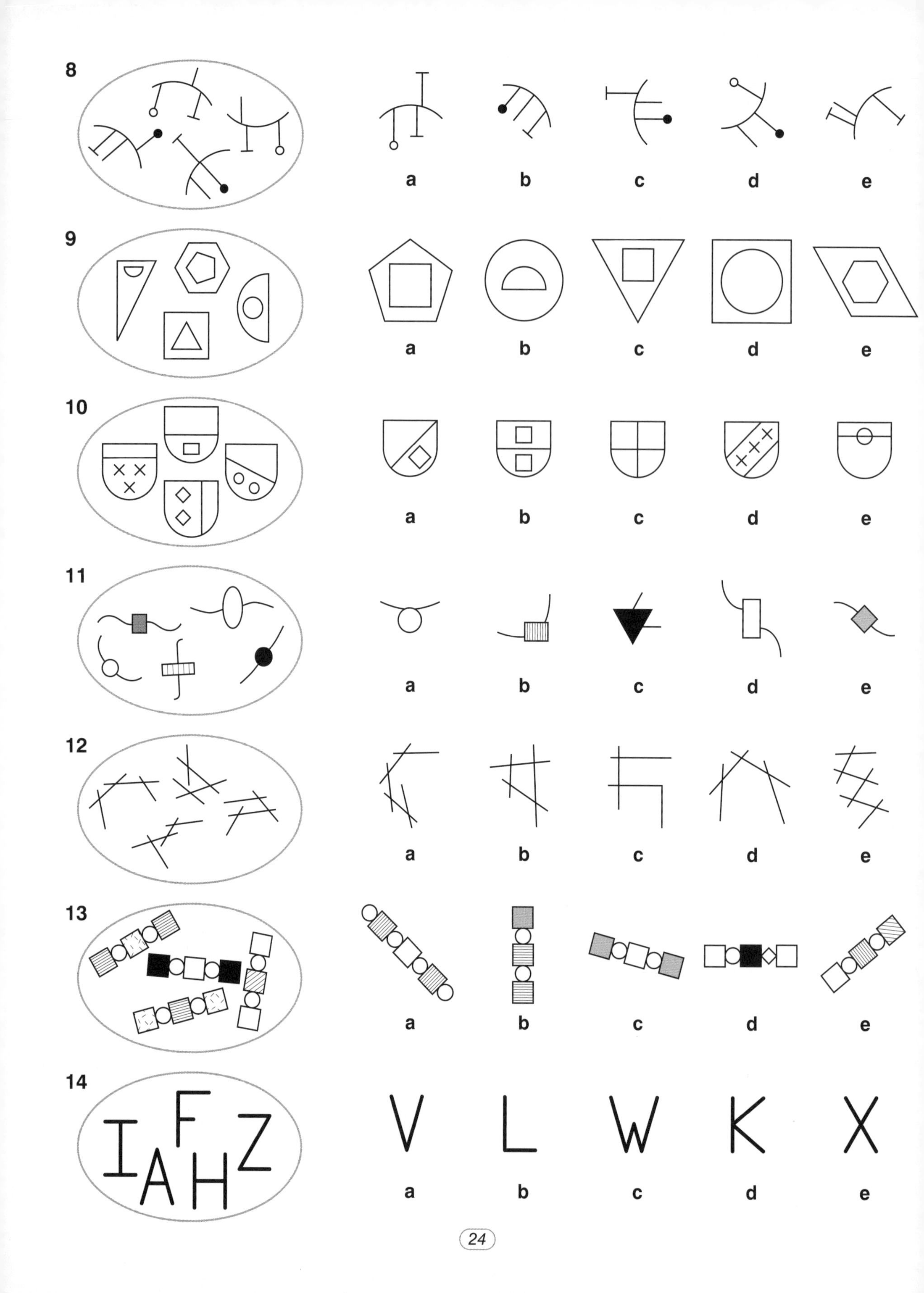
8
a
b
c
d
e
9
a
b
c
d
e
10
a
b
c
d
e
11
a
b
c
d
e
12
a
b
c
d
e
13
a
b
c
d
e
14
I F A H Z
V
a
L
b
W
c
K
d
X
e

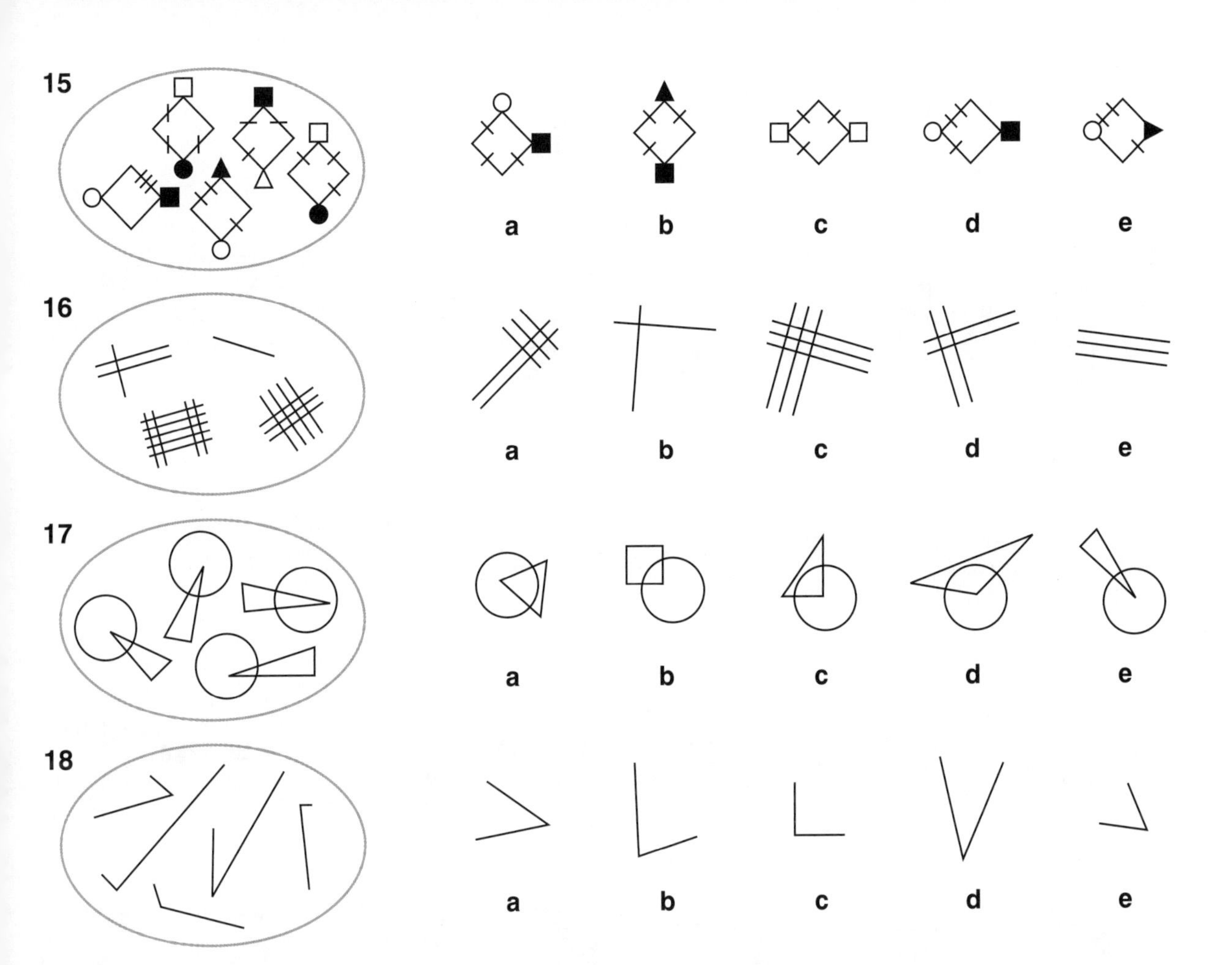

B 10 Which shape or pattern is made when the first two shapes or patterns are put together? Circle the letter.

Example

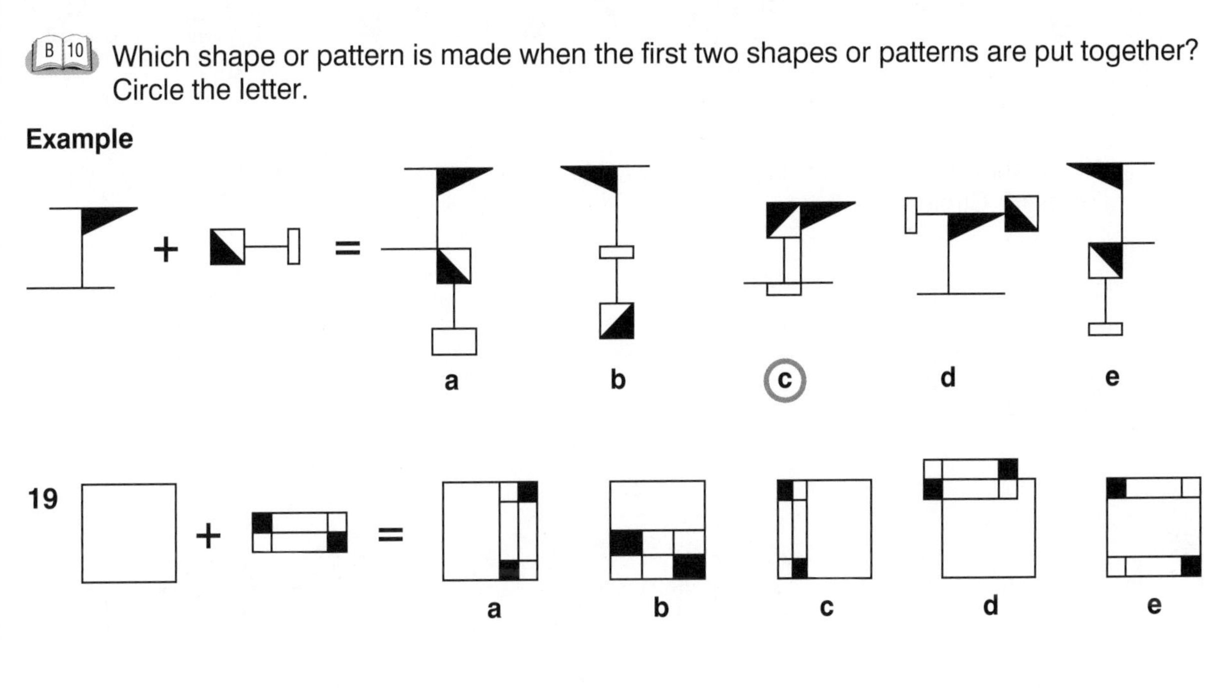

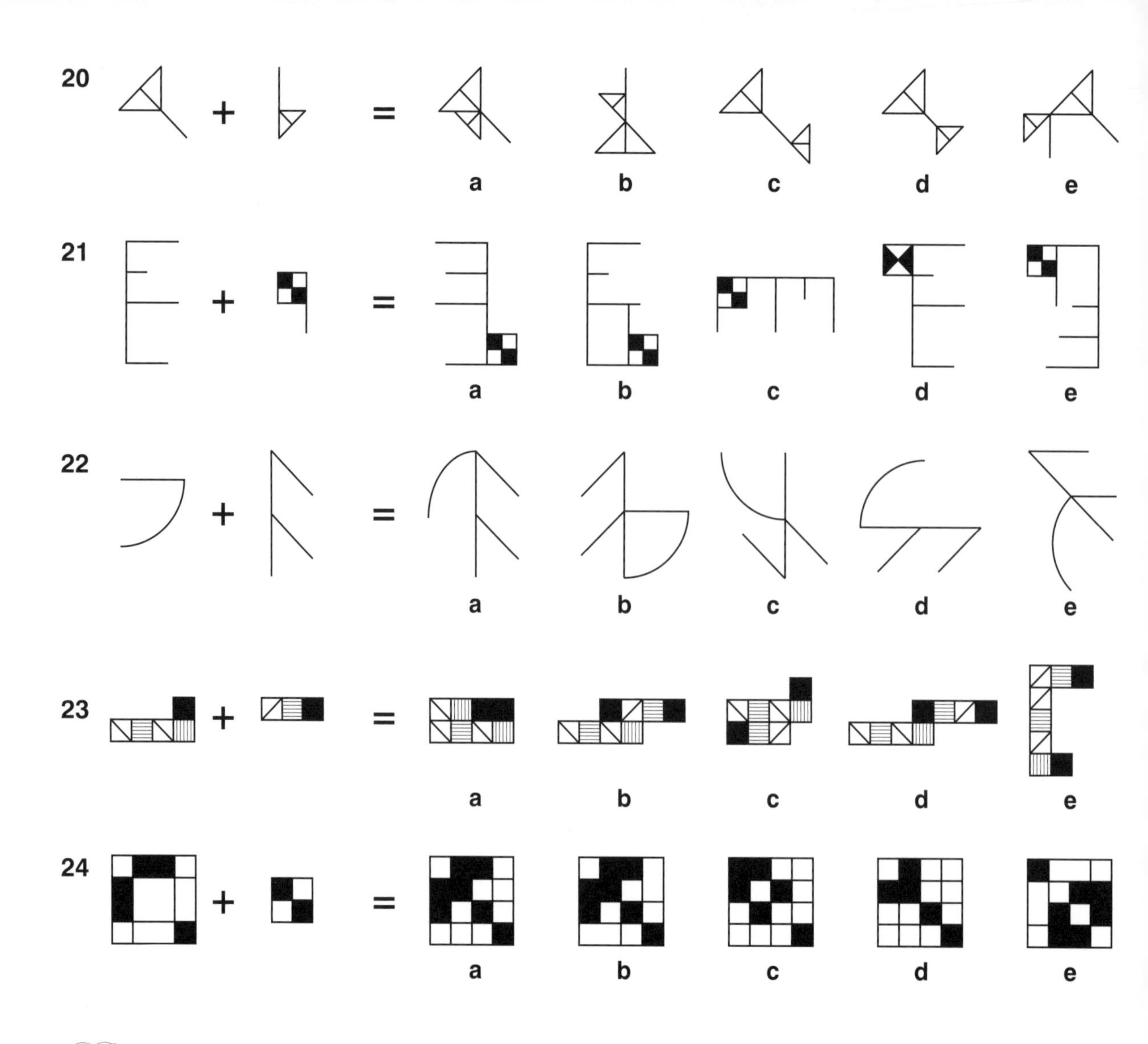

B 3 Which shape or pattern on the right completes the second pair in the same way as the first pair? Circle the letter.

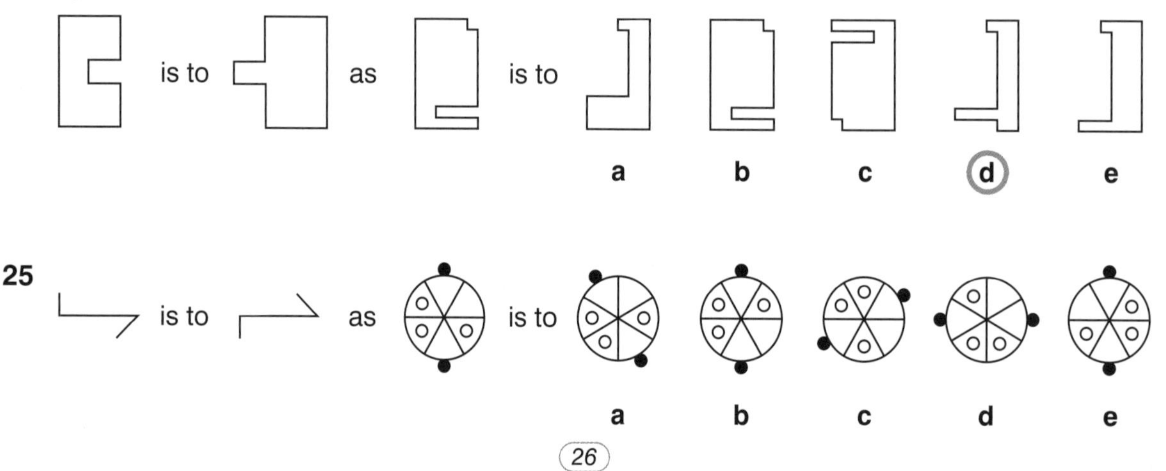

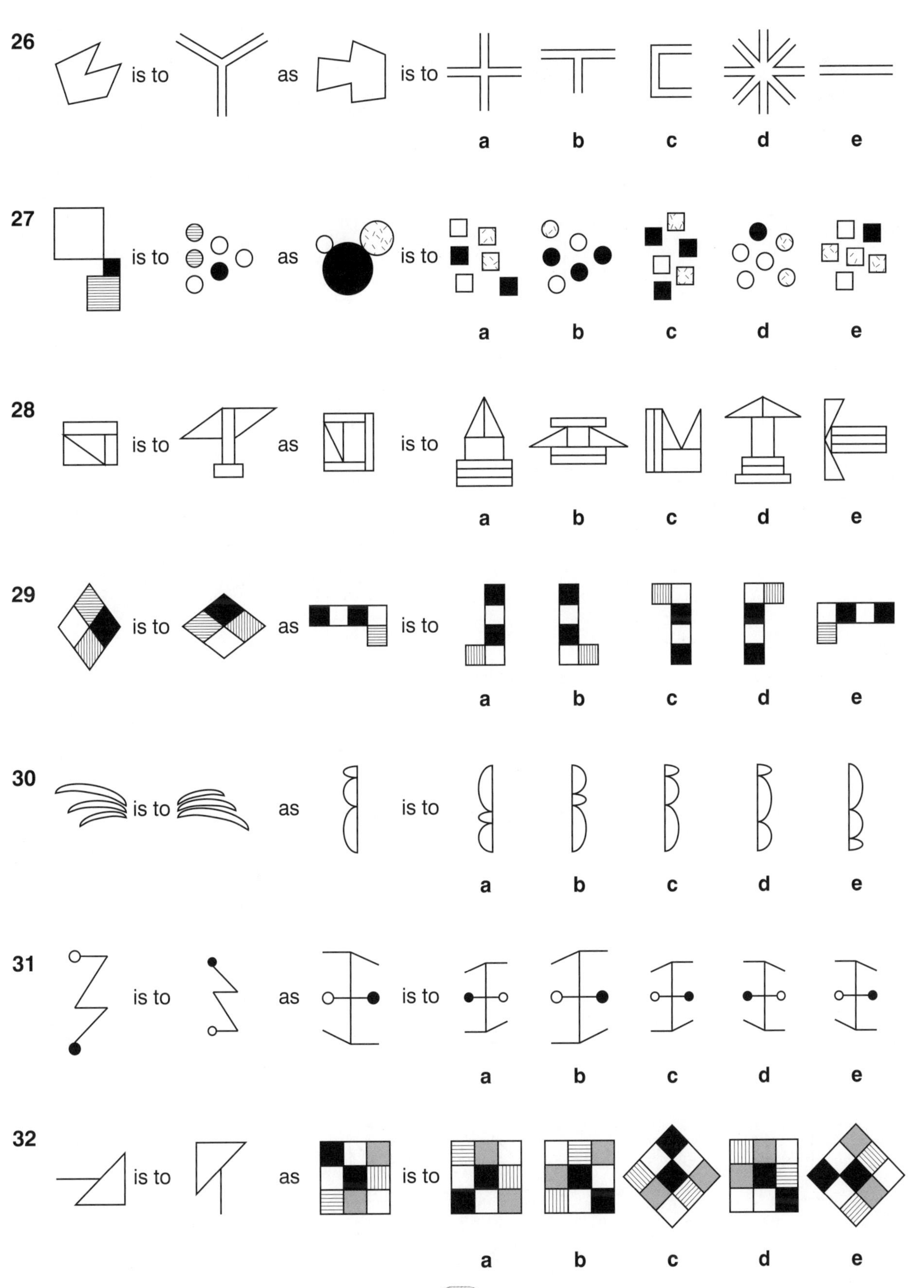
26
is to
as
is to
a
b
c
d
e
27
is to
as
is to
a
b
c
d
e
28
is to
as
is to
a
b
c
d
e
29
is to
as
is to
a
b
c
d
e
30
is to
as
is to
a
b
c
d
e
31
is to
as
is to
a
b
c
d
e
32
is to
as
is to
a
b
c
d
e

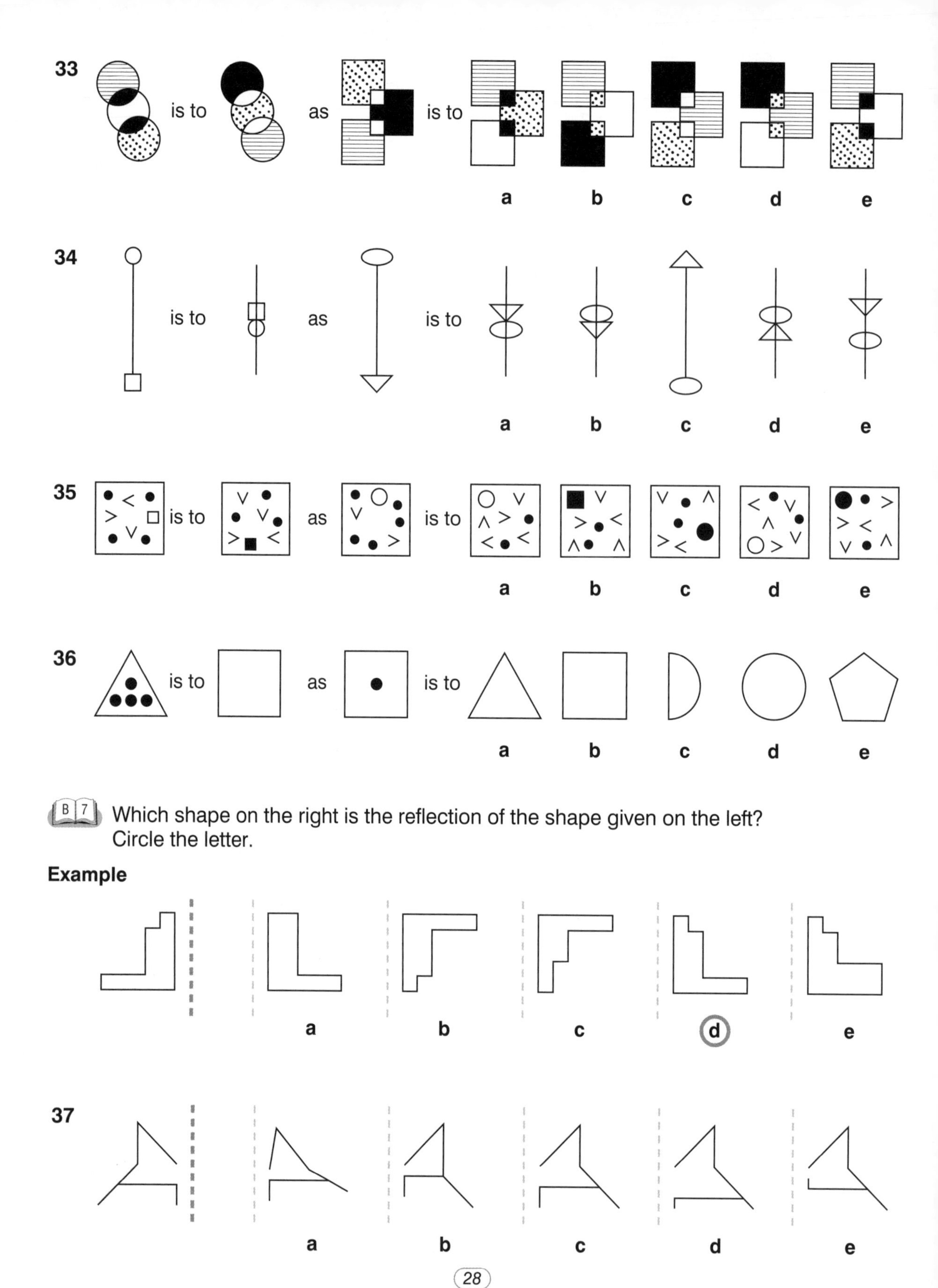
33
is to
as
is to
a
b
c
d
e
34
is to
as
is to
a
b
c
d
e
35
is to
as
is to
a
b
c
d
e
36
is to
as
is to
a
b
c
d
e
B 7
Which shape on the right is the reflection of the shape given on the left?
Circle the letter.
Example
a
b
c
d
e
37
a
b
c
d
e

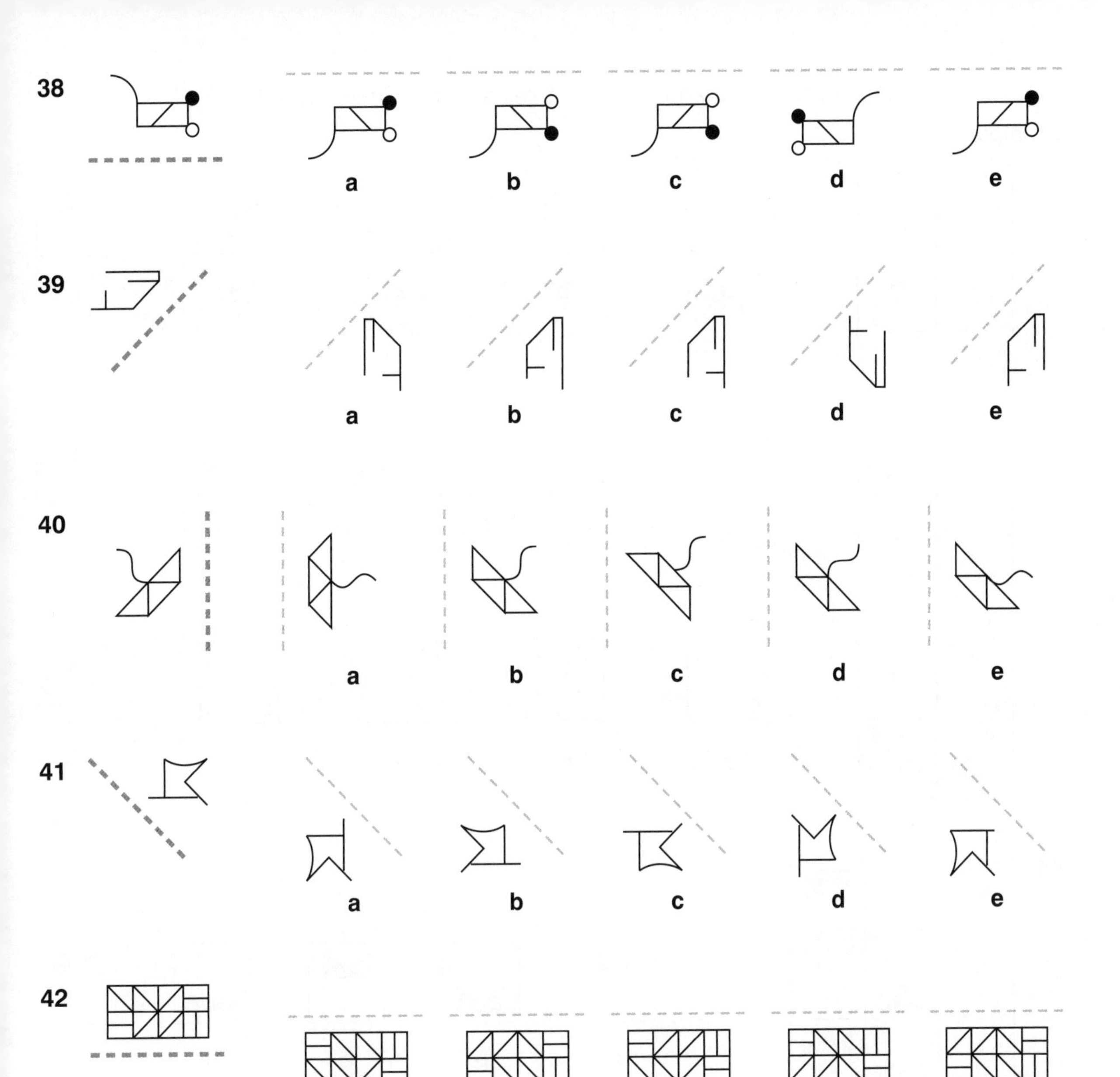
38
a
b
c
d
e
39
a
b
c
d
e
40
a
b
c
d
e
41
a
b
c
d
e
42
a
b
c
d
e

B 6 Which shape or pattern completes the larger square? Circle the letter.

Example

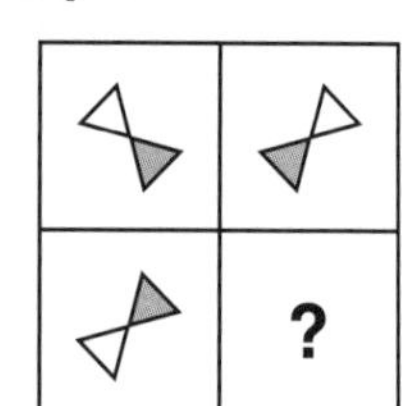

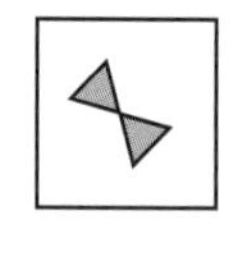
a

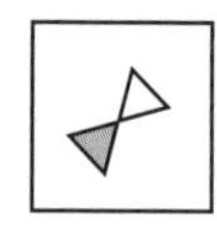
b

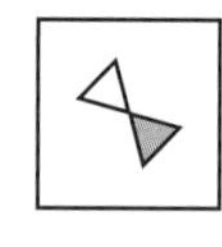
c

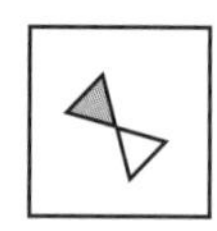
(d)

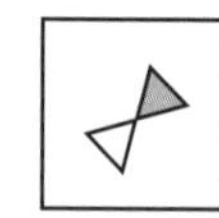
e

43

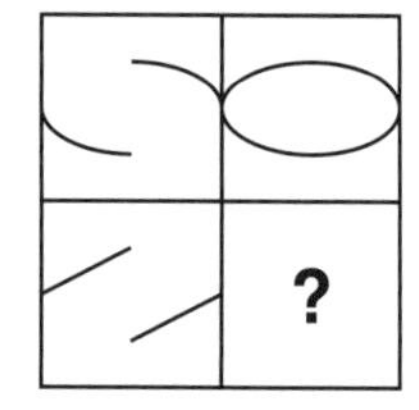

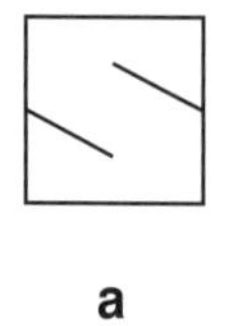
a

b

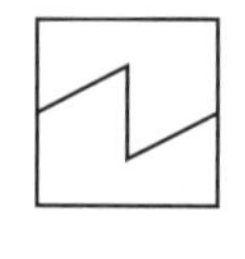
c

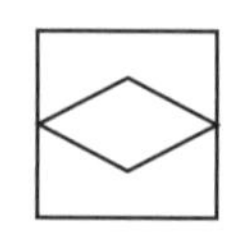
d

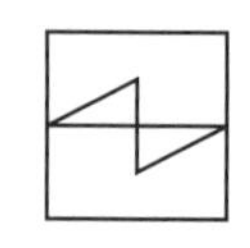
e

44

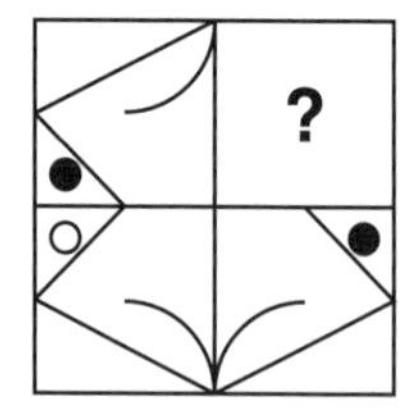

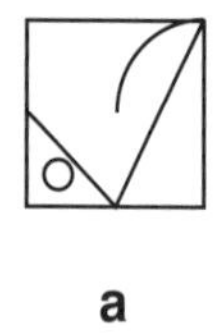
a

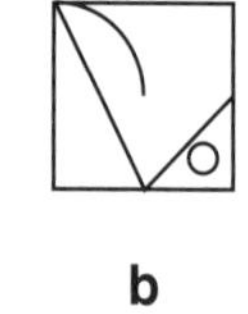
b

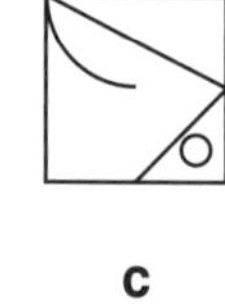
c

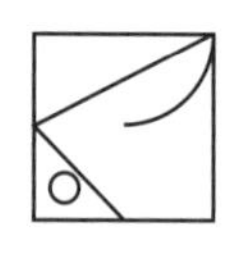
d

e

45

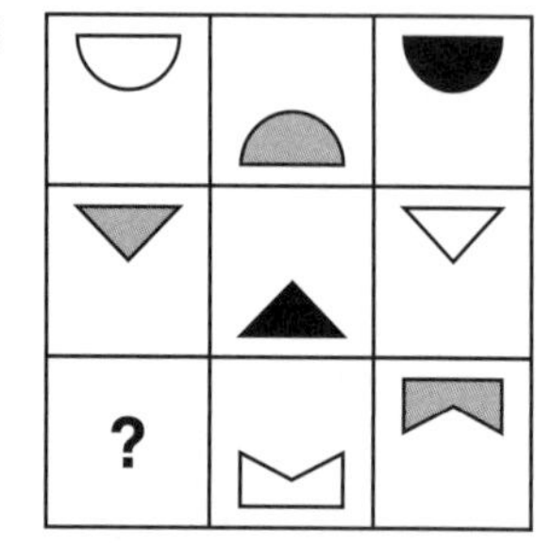

a

b

c

d

e

46

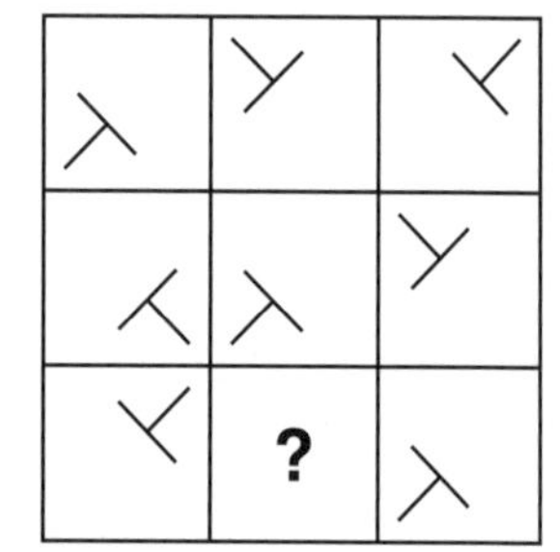

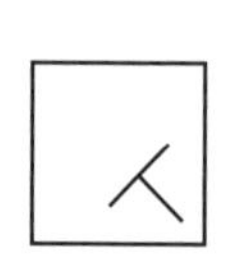
a

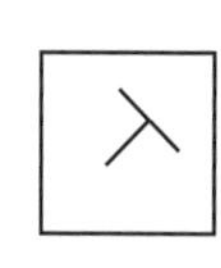
b

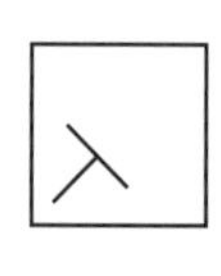
c

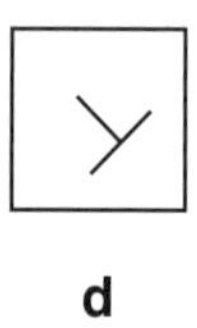
d

e

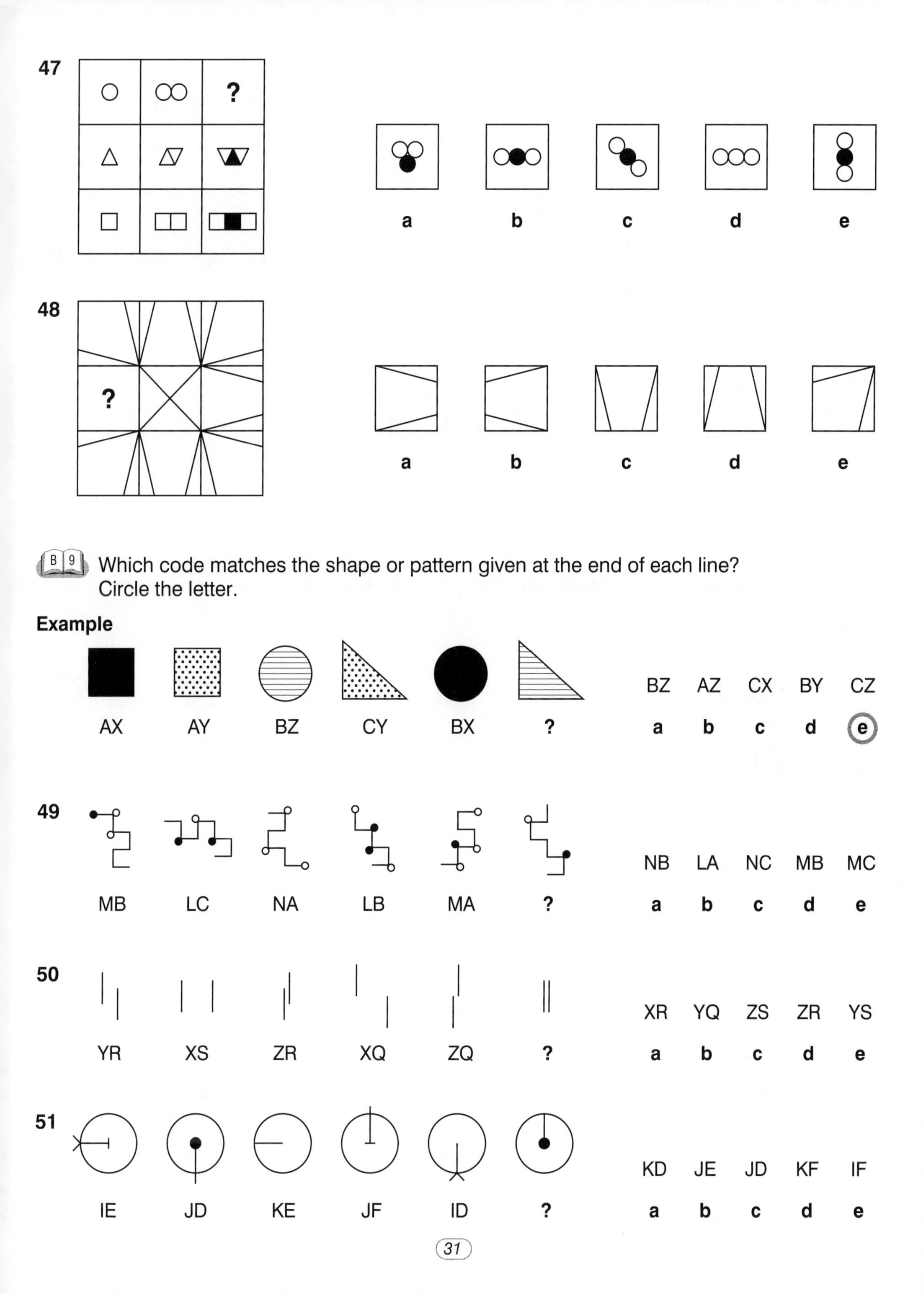
47
?
a
b
c
d
e
48
?
a
b
c
d
e
B 9
Which code matches the shape or pattern given at the end of each line? Circle the letter.
Example
AX
AY
BZ
CY
BX
?
BZ
AZ
CX
BY
CZ
a
b
c
d
e
49
MB
LC
NA
LB
MA
?
NB
LA
NC
MB
MC
a
b
c
d
e
50
YR
XS
ZR
XQ
ZQ
?
XR
YQ
ZS
ZR
YS
a
b
c
d
e
51
IE
JD
KE
JF
ID
?
KD
JE
JD
KF
IF
a
b
c
d
e
31

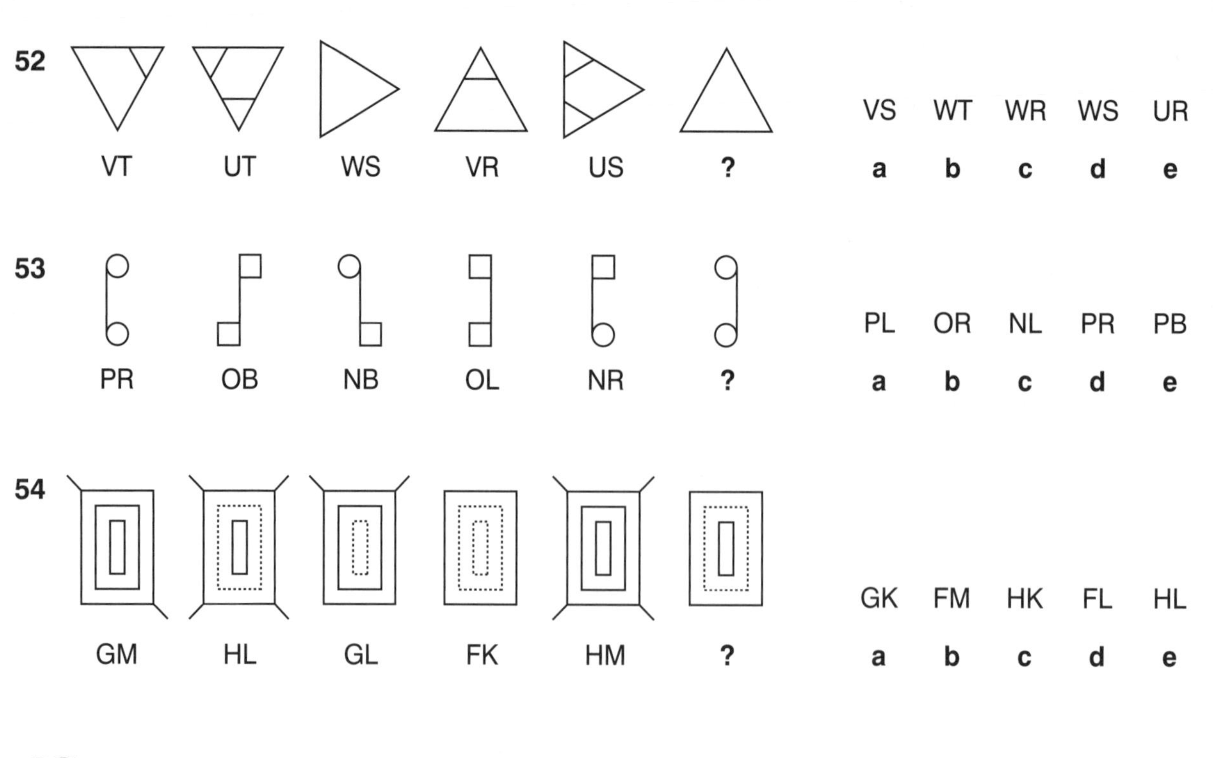

B8 Which cube cannot be made from the given net? Circle the letter.

Example

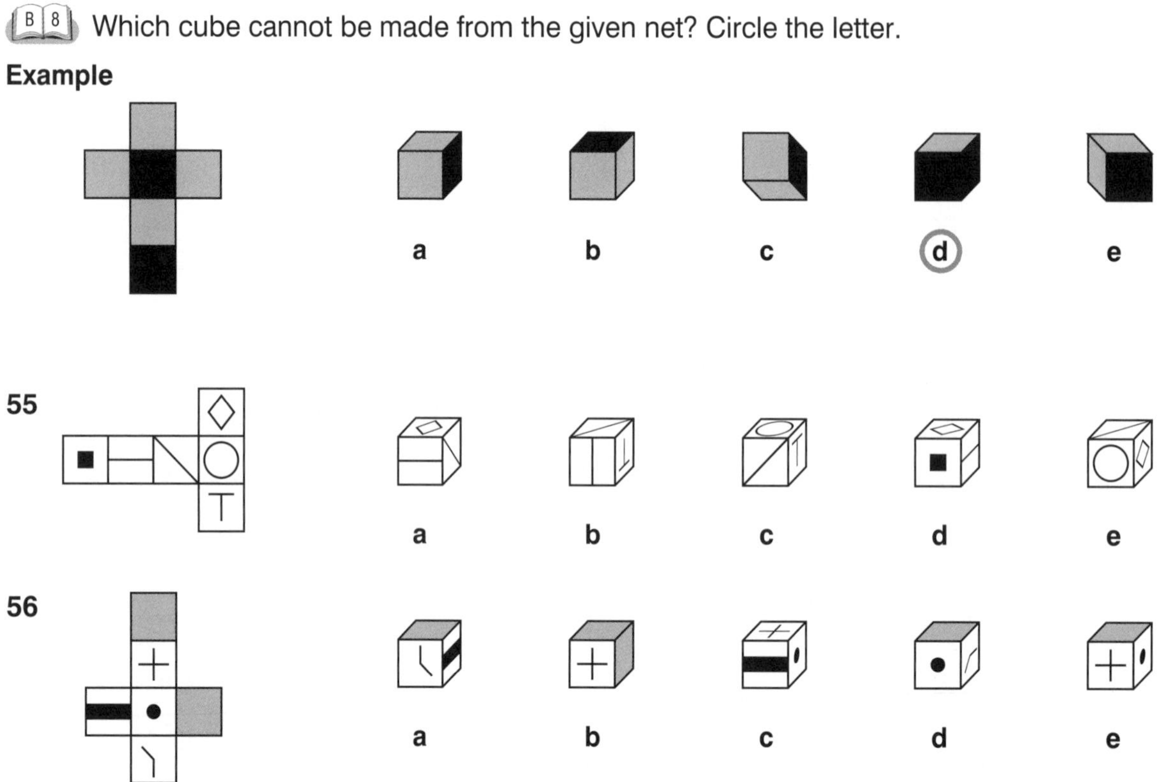

Paper 1

1	b	31	b
2	e	32	e
3	c	33	c
4	a	34	e
5	d	35	a
6	d	36	d
7	e	37	b
8	b	38	e
9	d	39	e
10	a	40	c
11	c	41	a
12	c	42	d
13	d	43	a
14	c	44	d
15	e	45	a
16	b	46	c
17	c	47	e
18	c	48	b
19	d	49	c
20	c	50	a
21	d	51	b
22	a	52	e
23	e	53	c
24	a	54	d
25	c	55	a
26	b	56	a
27	b	57	c
28	e	58	b
29	d	59	d
30	a	60	d

Paper 2

1	e	31	e
2	b	32	b
3	b	33	a
4	c	34	e
5	d	35	d
6	c	36	c
7	a	37	a
8	e	38	e
9	a	39	e
10	b	40	d
11	d	41	b
12	c	42	c
13	b	43	b
14	e	44	a
15	d	45	b
16	b	46	d
17	a	47	e
18	d	48	e
19	c	49	c
20	c	50	a
21	e	51	d
22	b	52	d
23	d	53	c
24	a	54	a
25	c	55	b
26	d	56	b
27	d	57	e
28	b	58	b
29	e	59	c
30	c	60	d

Paper 3

1	b	31	c
2	c	32	b
3	a	33	b
4	d	34	a
5	e	35	e
6	e	36	d
7	c	37	c
8	c	38	b
9	a	39	e
10	a	40	b
11	e	41	a
12	d	42	d
13	c	43	d
14	d	44	c
15	d	45	e
16	a	46	a
17	e	47	b
18	b	48	b
19	a	49	e
20	c	50	c
21	b	51	d
22	d	52	c
23	c	53	a
24	e	54	d
25	b	55	b
26	a	56	a
27	c	57	e
28	d	58	e
29	c	59	c
30	e	60	d

Paper 4

1	b	31	e
2	e	32	b
3	a	33	c
4	d	34	a
5	a	35	d
6	e	36	d
7	c	37	a
8	c	38	c
9	b	39	e
10	b	40	d
11	e	41	b
12	b	42	b
13	b	43	b
14	e	44	d
15	c	45	c
16	e	46	d
17	d	47	a
18	a	48	e
19	d	49	c
20	c	50	b
21	b	51	d
22	a	52	d
23	e	53	a
24	c	54	d
25	c	55	b
26	d	56	b
27	b	57	a
28	d	58	b
29	a	59	c
30	a	60	a

Paper 5

1	e	31	d
2	b	32	a
3	b	33	c
4	c	34	b
5	a	35	c
6	d	36	e
7	b	37	b
8	d	38	b
9	e	39	b
10	e	40	a
11	c	41	c
12	a	42	c
13	e	43	d
14	c	44	e
15	a	45	b
16	b	46	a
17	a	47	c
18	b	48	e
19	e	49	b
20	a	50	e
21	a	51	a
22	c	52	c
23	b	53	b
24	b	54	d
25	e	55	a
26	e	56	a
27	b	57	b
28	a	58	e
29	c	59	c
30	d	60	e

Paper 6

1	a	31	d
2	b	32	c
3	e	33	a
4	a	34	e
5	b	35	e
6	c	36	b
7	d	37	b
8	c	38	c
9	e	39	e
10	b	40	e
11	d	41	a
12	c	42	d
13	a	43	c
14	b	44	b
15	a	45	e
16	d	46	d
17	c	47	a
18	e	48	a
19	b	49	c
20	a	50	e
21	c	51	a
22	c	52	b
23	d	53	c
24	c	54	d
25	e	55	b
26	e	56	e
27	c	57	a
28	a	58	d
29	b	59	c
30	d	60	c

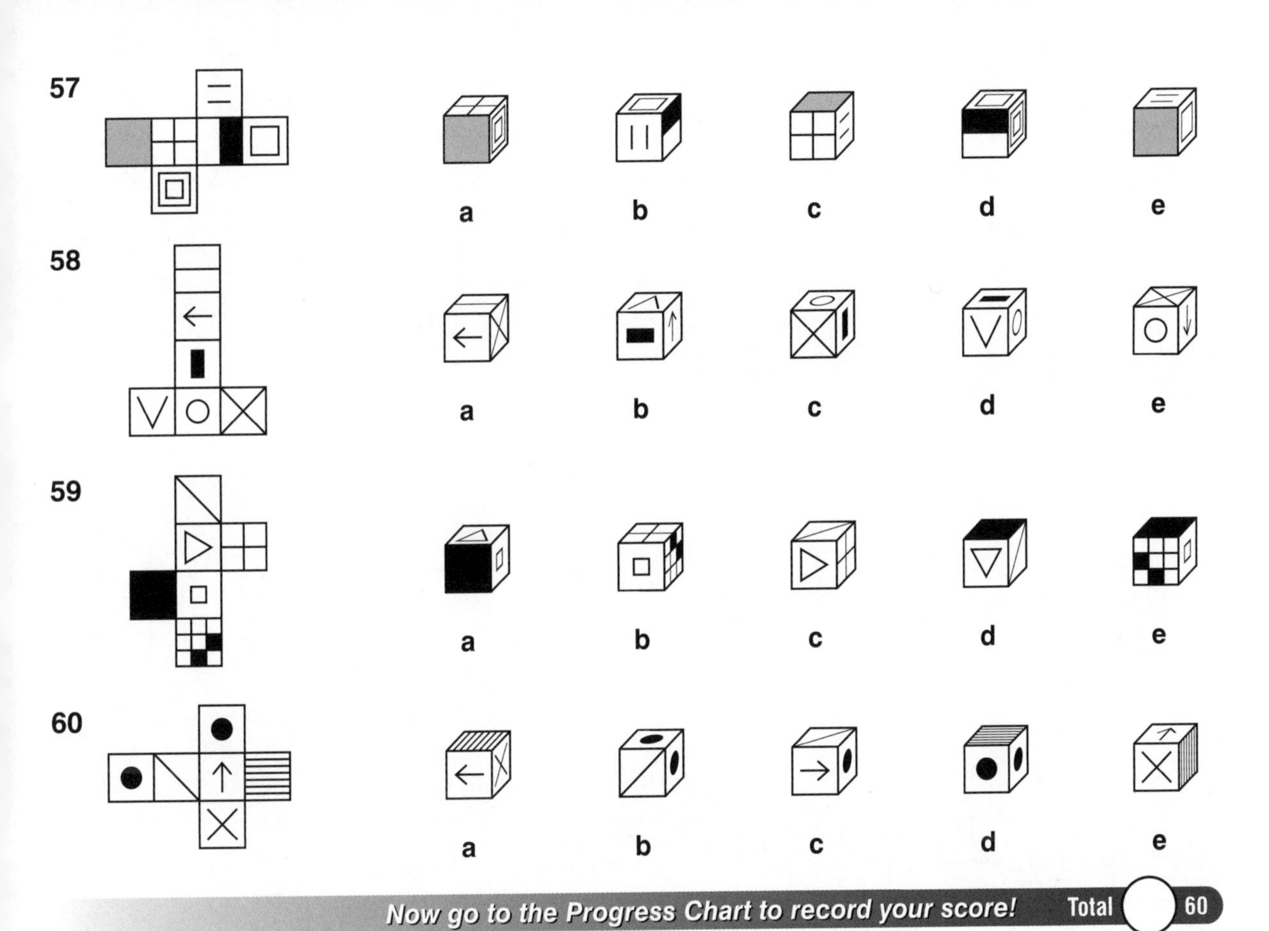

Paper 4

B 2 Which pattern on the right belongs in the group on the left? Circle the letter.

Example

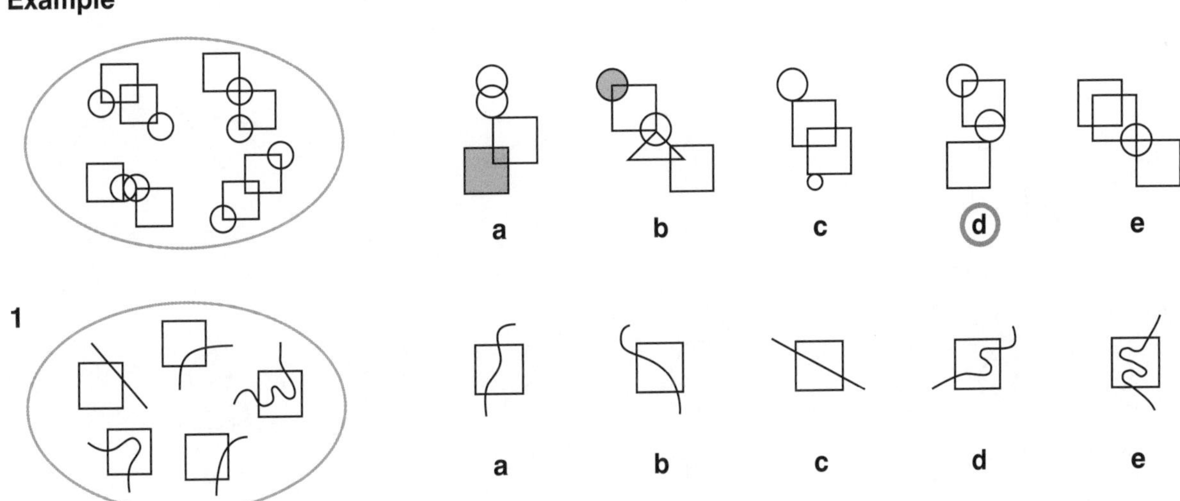

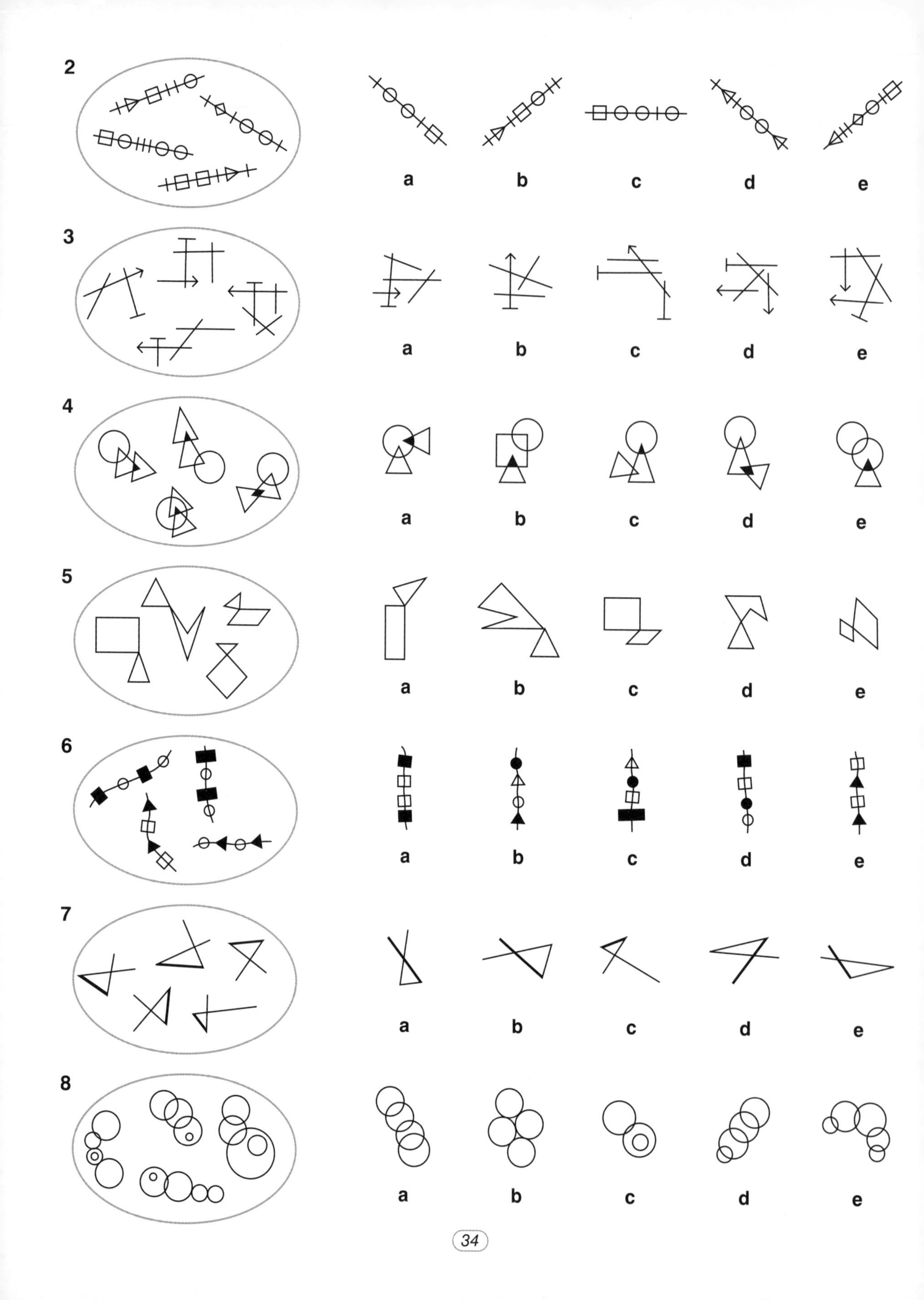
2
a b c d e
3
a b c d e
4
a b c d e
5
a b c d e
6
a b c d e
7
a b c d e
8
a b c d e

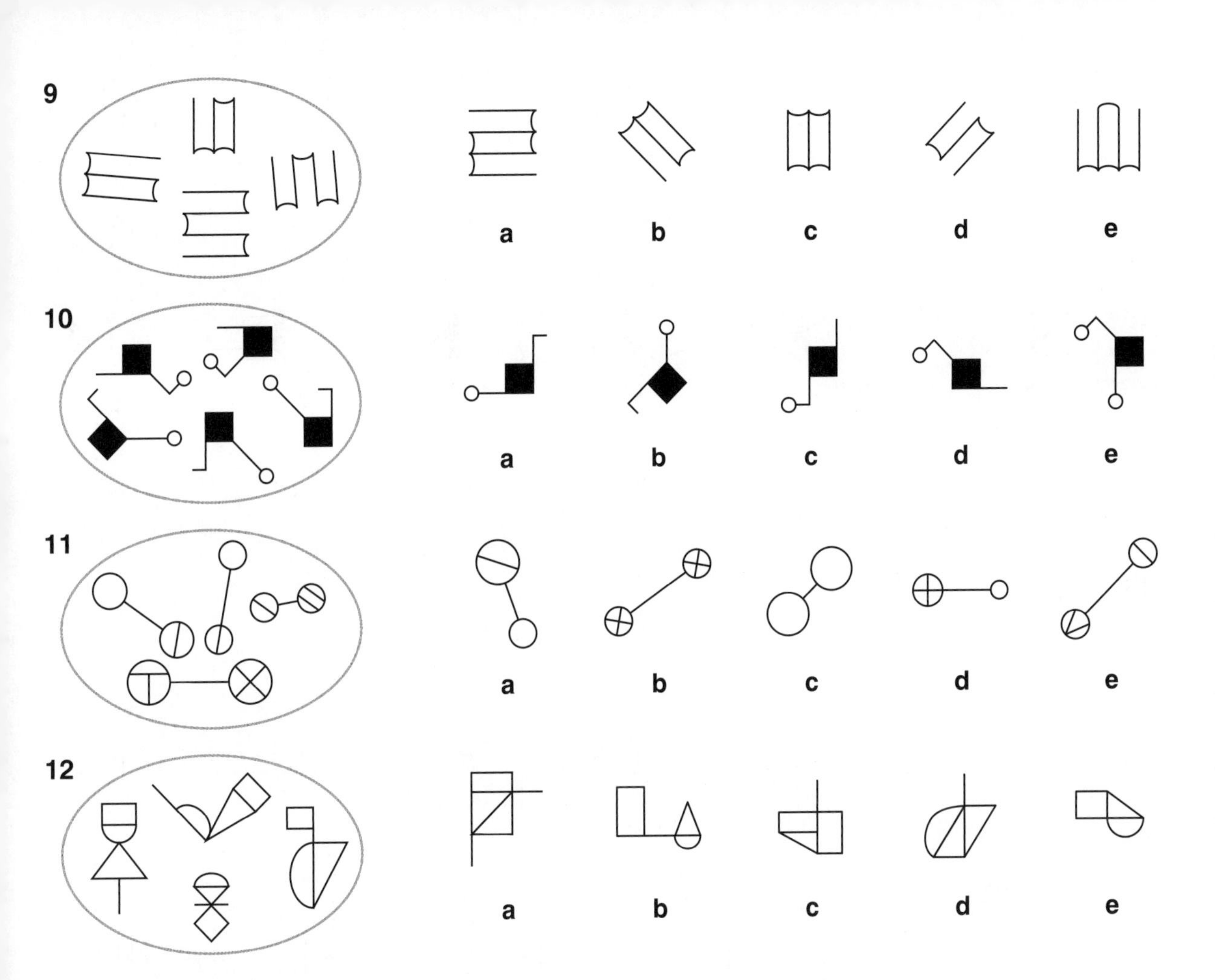

B7 Which shape on the right is the reflection of the shape given on the left? Circle the letter.

Example

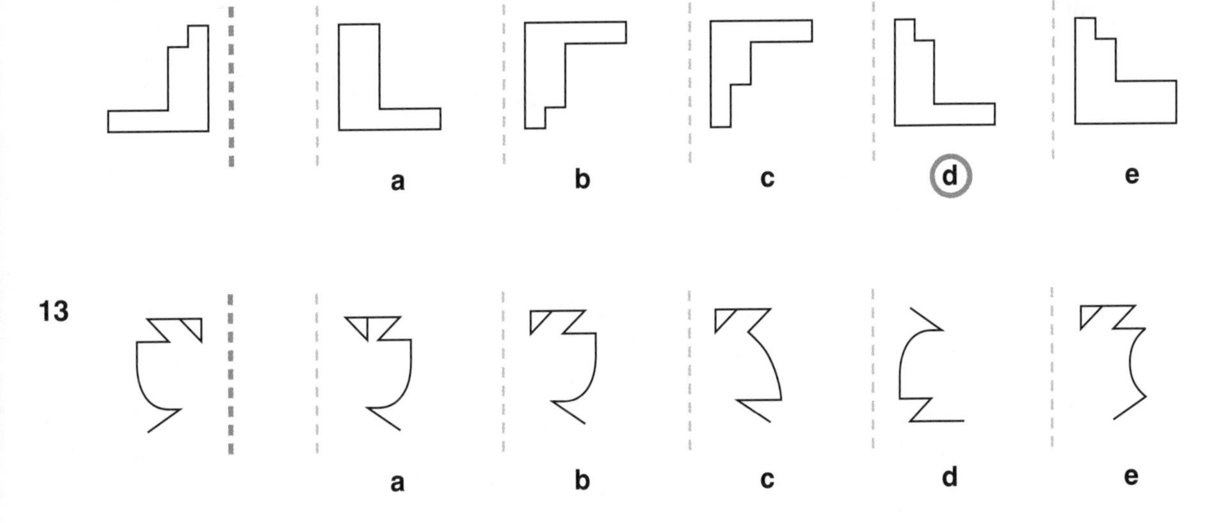

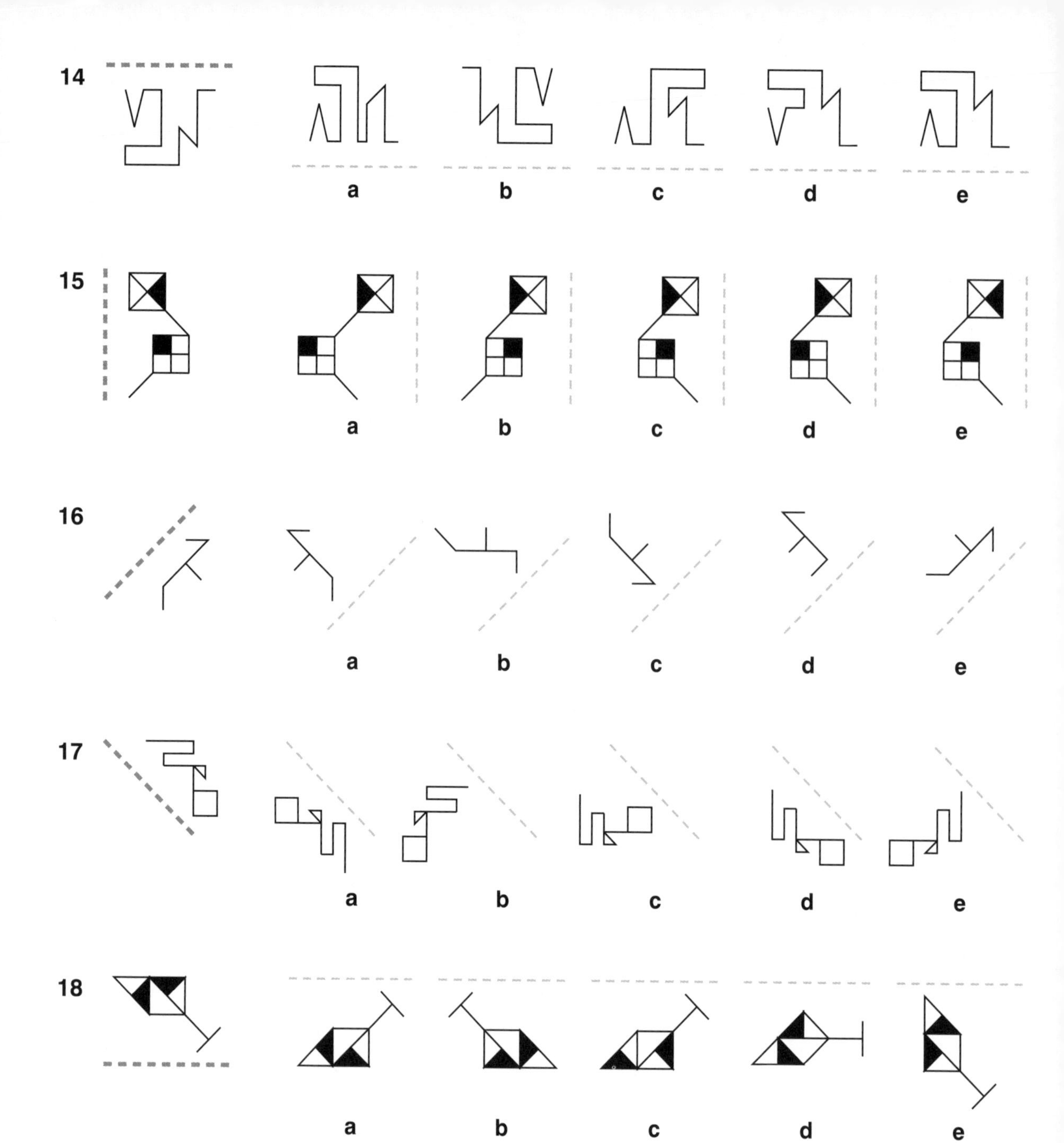
14
a
b
c
d
e
15
a
b
c
d
e
16
a
b
c
d
e
17
a
b
c
d
e
18
a
b
c
d
e

Which one comes next? Circle the letter.

Example

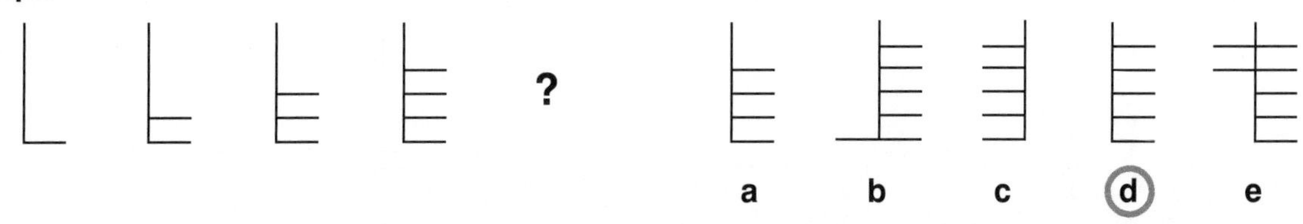

19

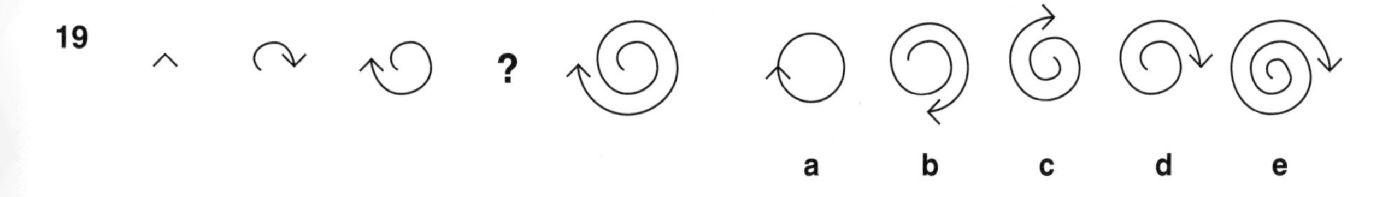

20

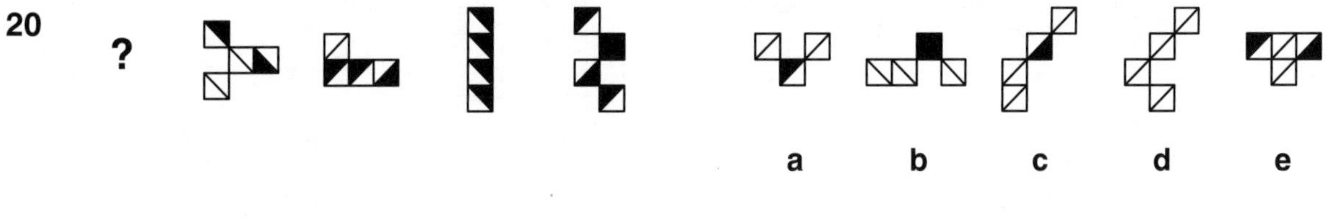

21

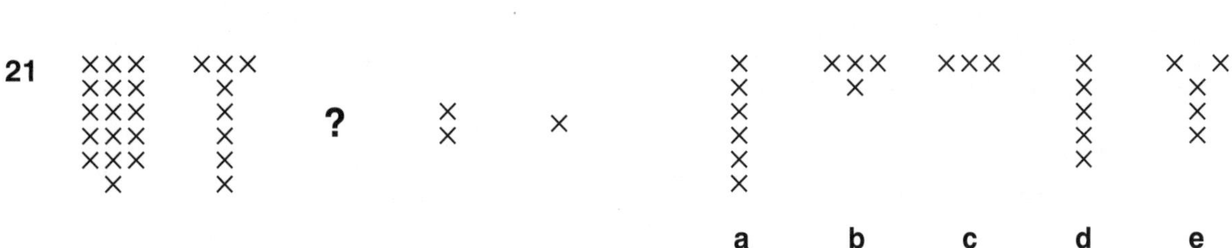

22

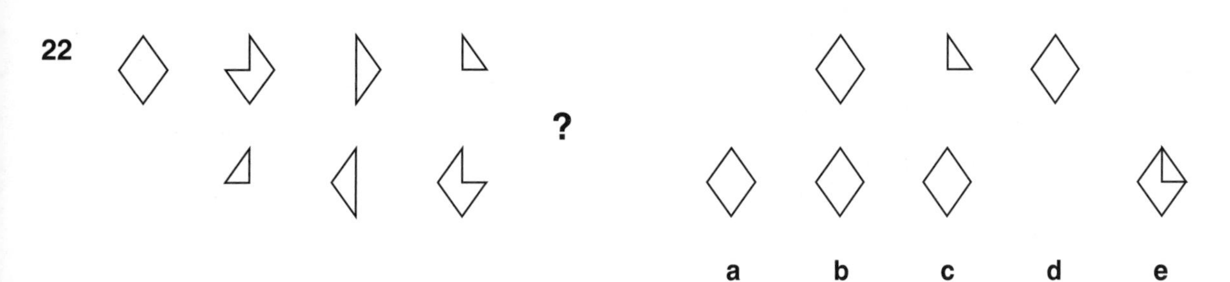

23

?

a b c d e

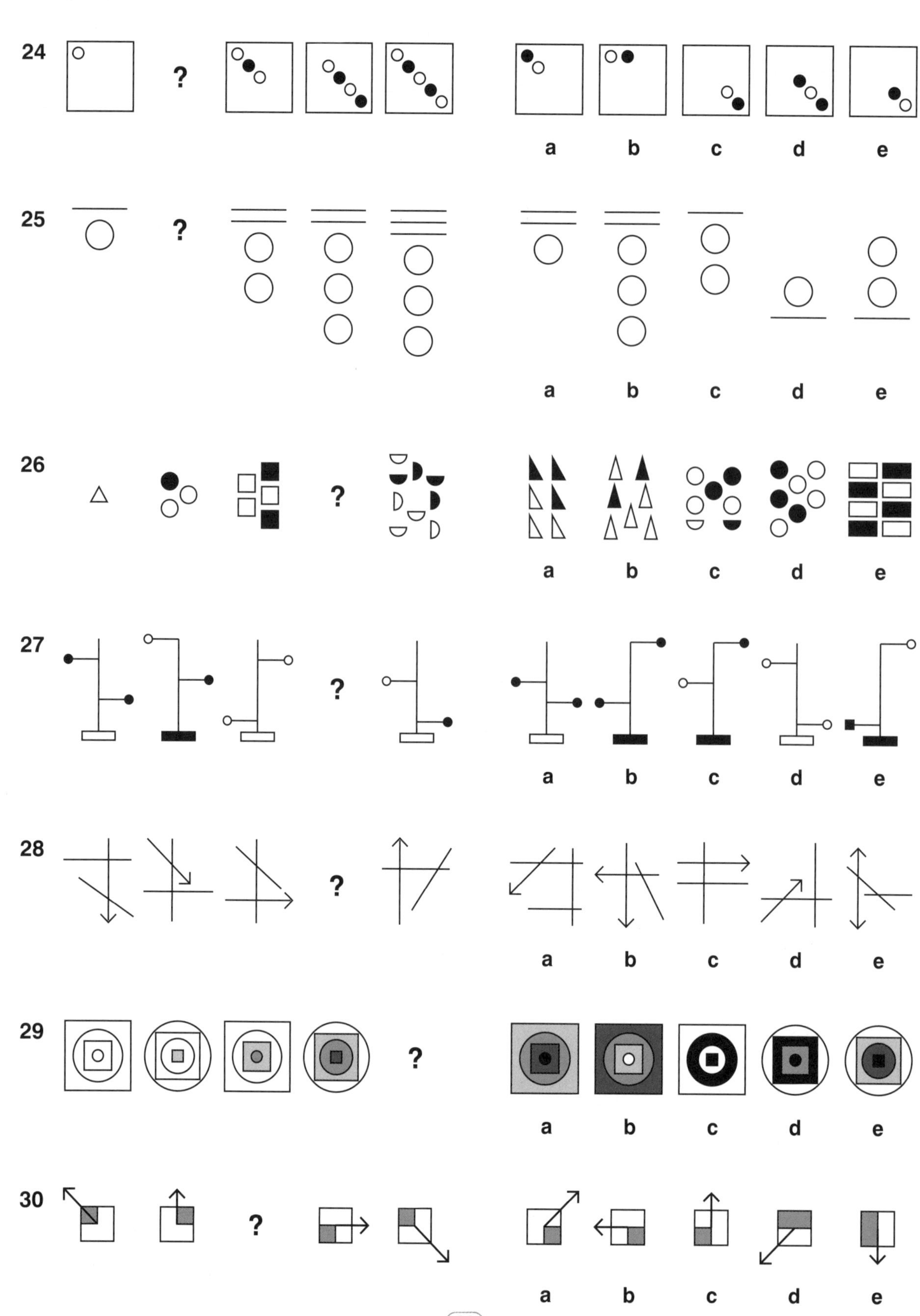
24
?
a
b
c
d
e
25
?
a
b
c
d
e
26
?
a
b
c
d
e
27
?
a
b
c
d
e
28
?
a
b
c
d
e
29
?
a
b
c
d
e
30
?
a
b
c
d
e

Which shape or pattern completes the larger square? Circle the letter.

Example

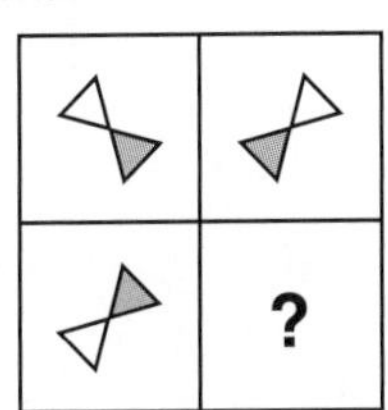

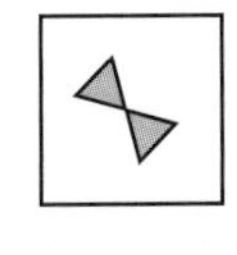

a

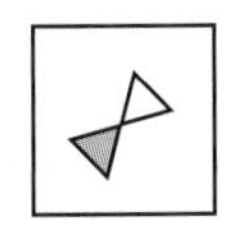

b

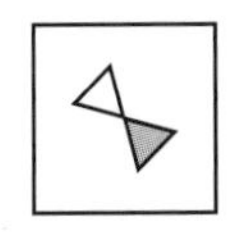

c

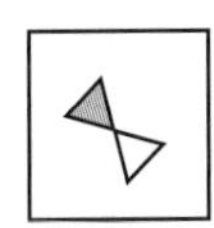

d

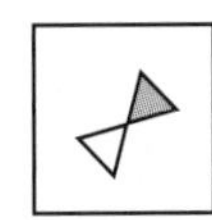

e

31

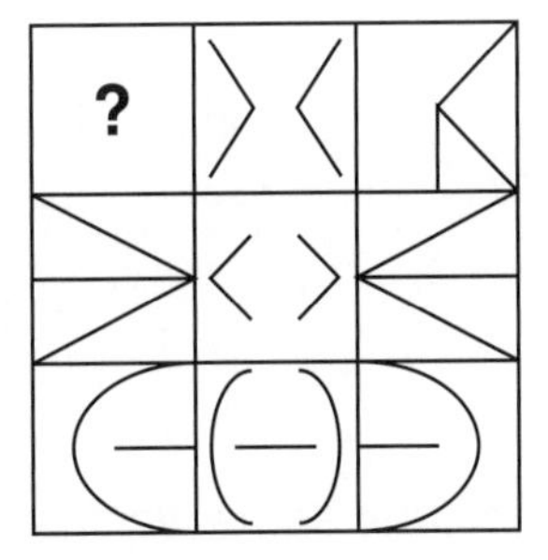

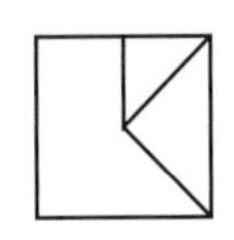

a

b

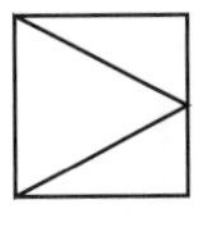

c

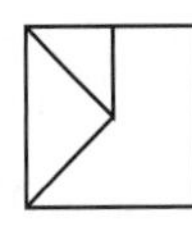

d

e

32

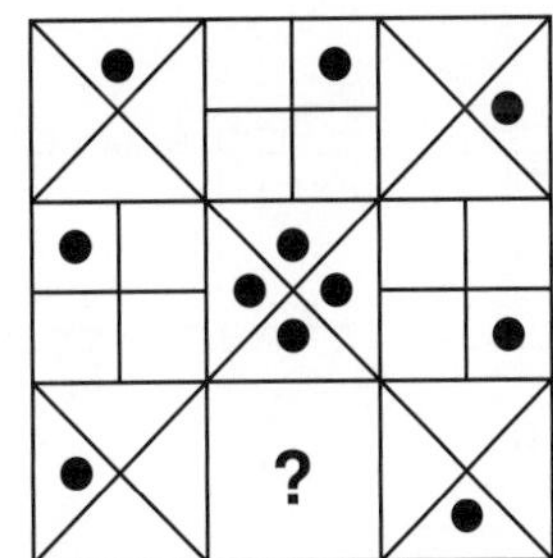

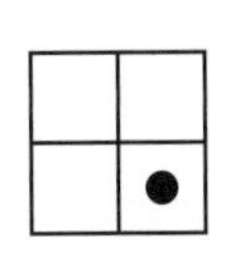

a

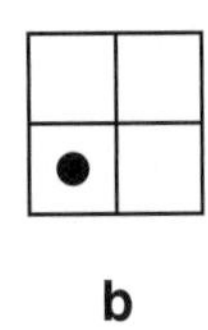

b

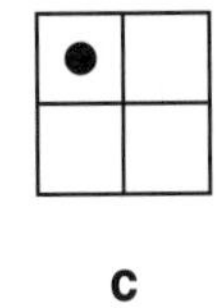

c

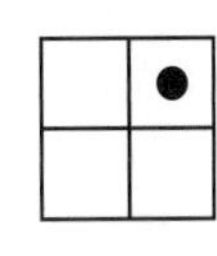

d

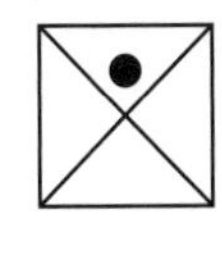

e

33

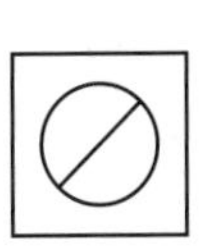

a

b

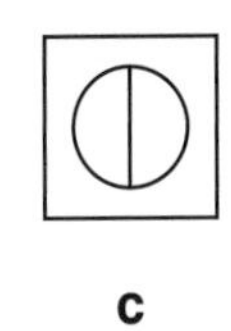

c

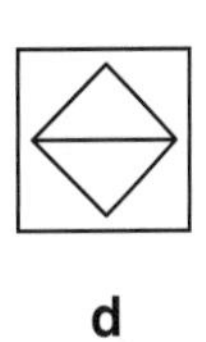

d

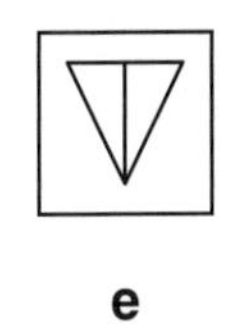

e

34

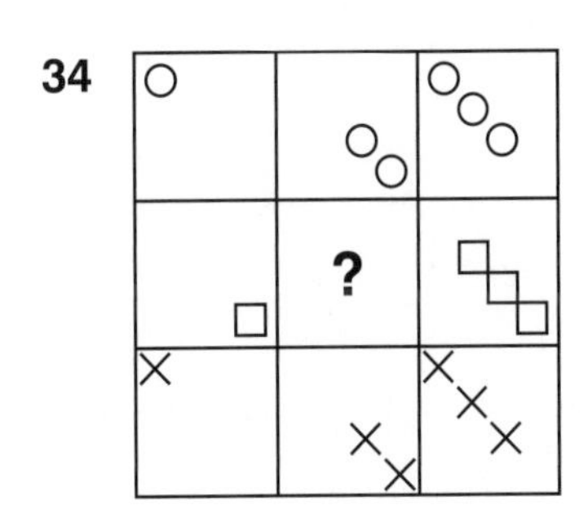

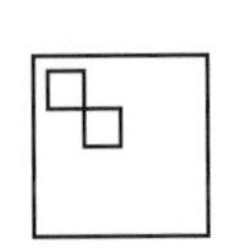

a

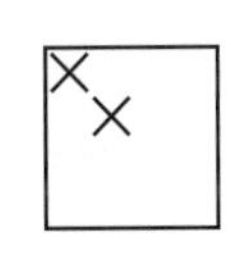

b

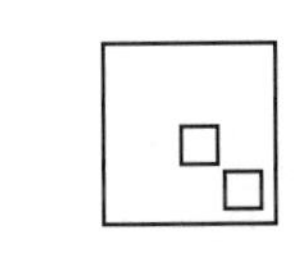

c

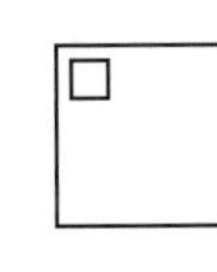

d

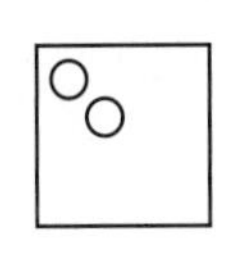

e

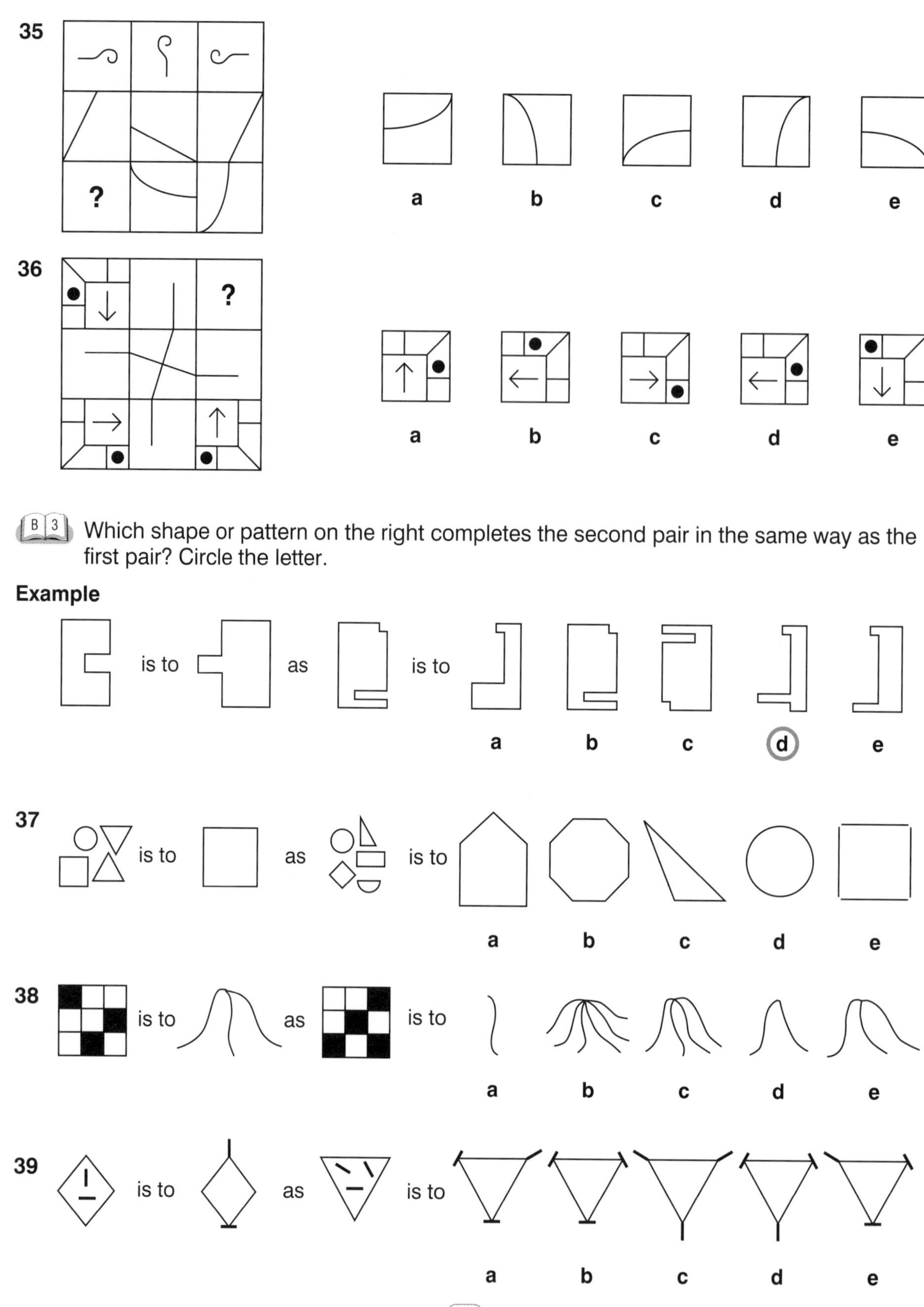
35
?
a
b
c
d
e
36
?
a
b
c
d
e
B 3
Which shape or pattern on the right completes the second pair in the same way as the first pair? Circle the letter.
Example
is to
as
is to
a
b
c
d
e
37
is to
as
is to
a
b
c
d
e
38
is to
as
is to
a
b
c
d
e
39
is to
as
is to
a
b
c
d
e

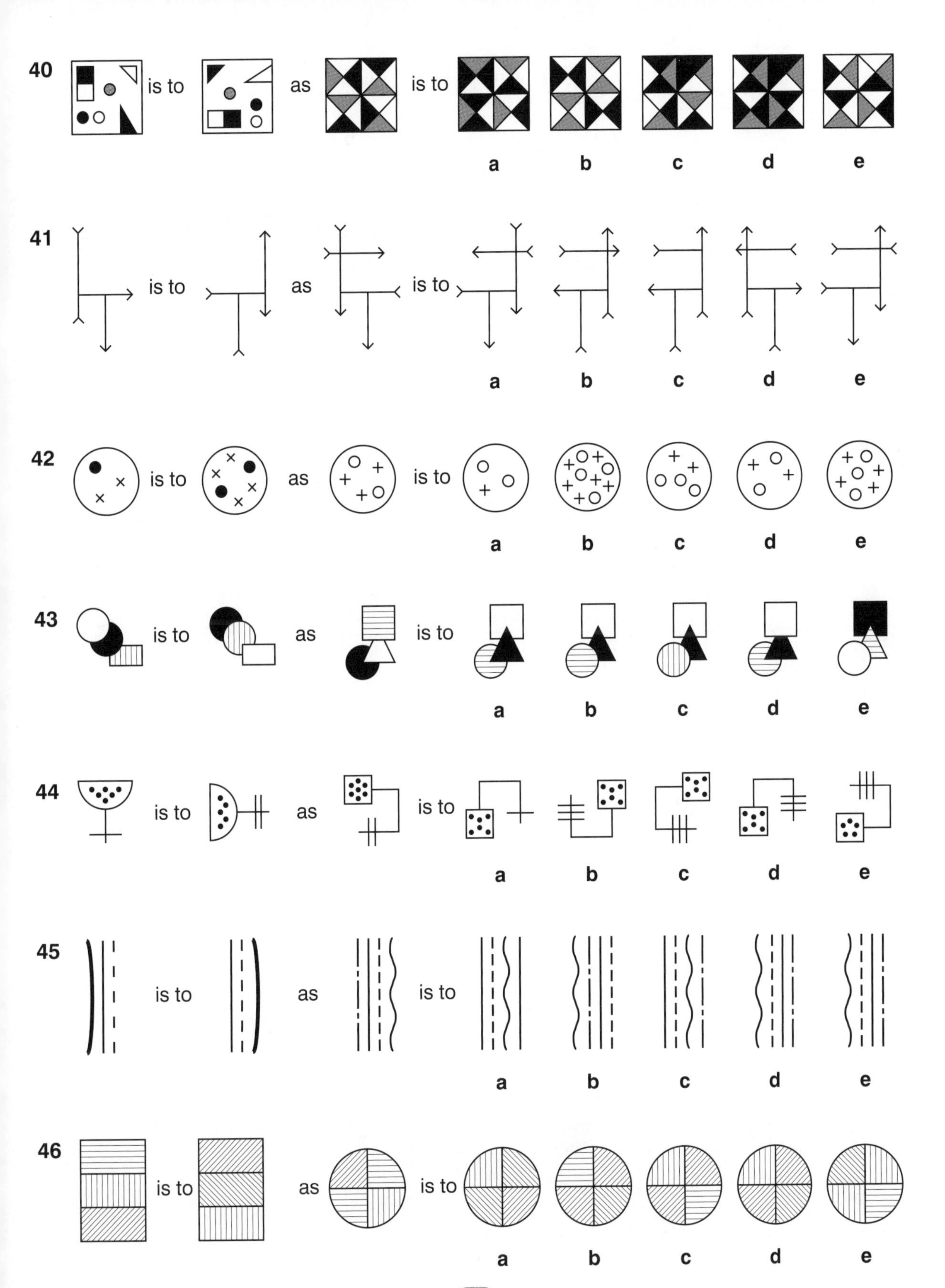
40
is to
as
is to
a
b
c
d
e
41
is to
as
is to
a
b
c
d
e
42
is to
as
is to
a
b
c
d
e
43
is to
as
is to
a
b
c
d
e
44
is to
as
is to
a
b
c
d
e
45
is to
as
is to
a
b
c
d
e
46
is to
as
is to
a
b
c
d
e

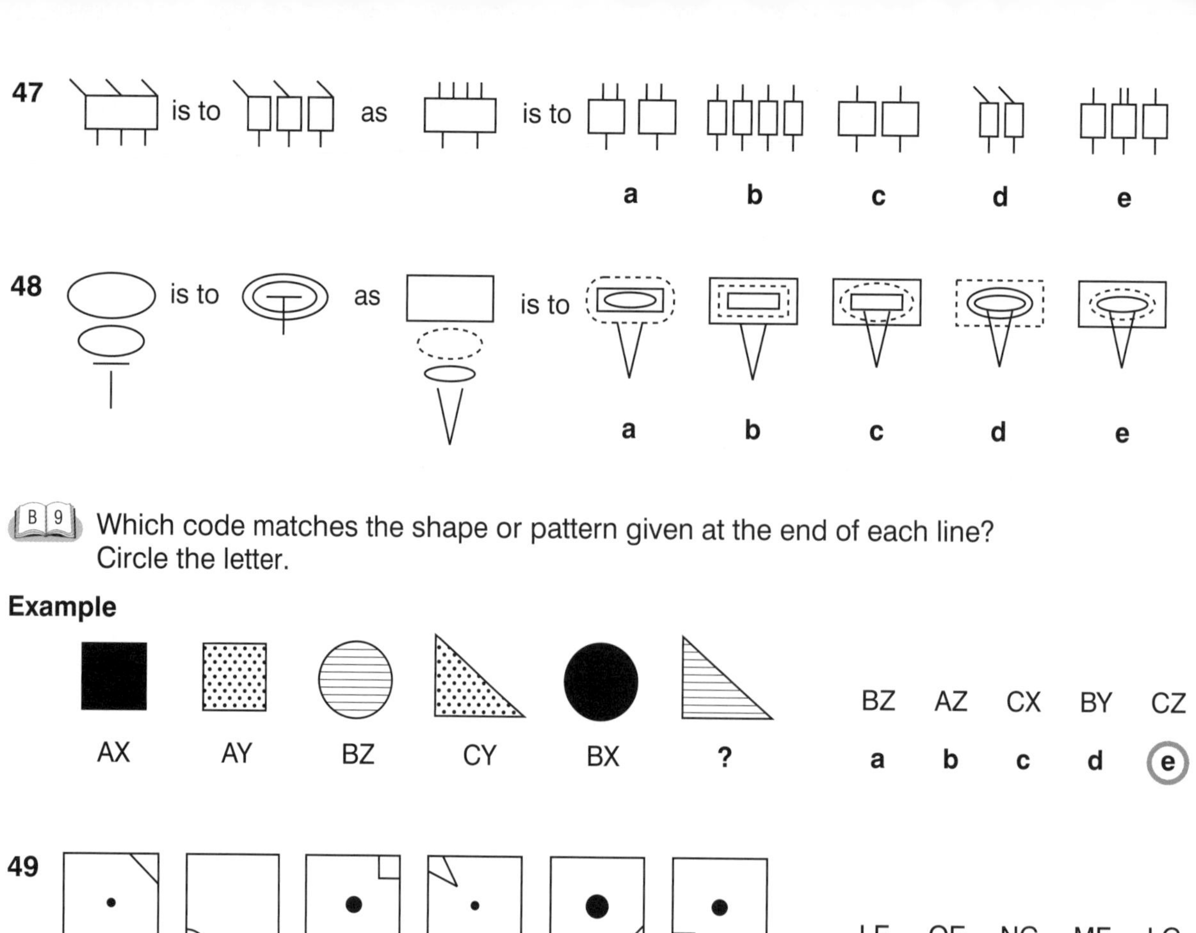

Which code matches the shape or pattern given at the end of each line? Circle the letter.

Example

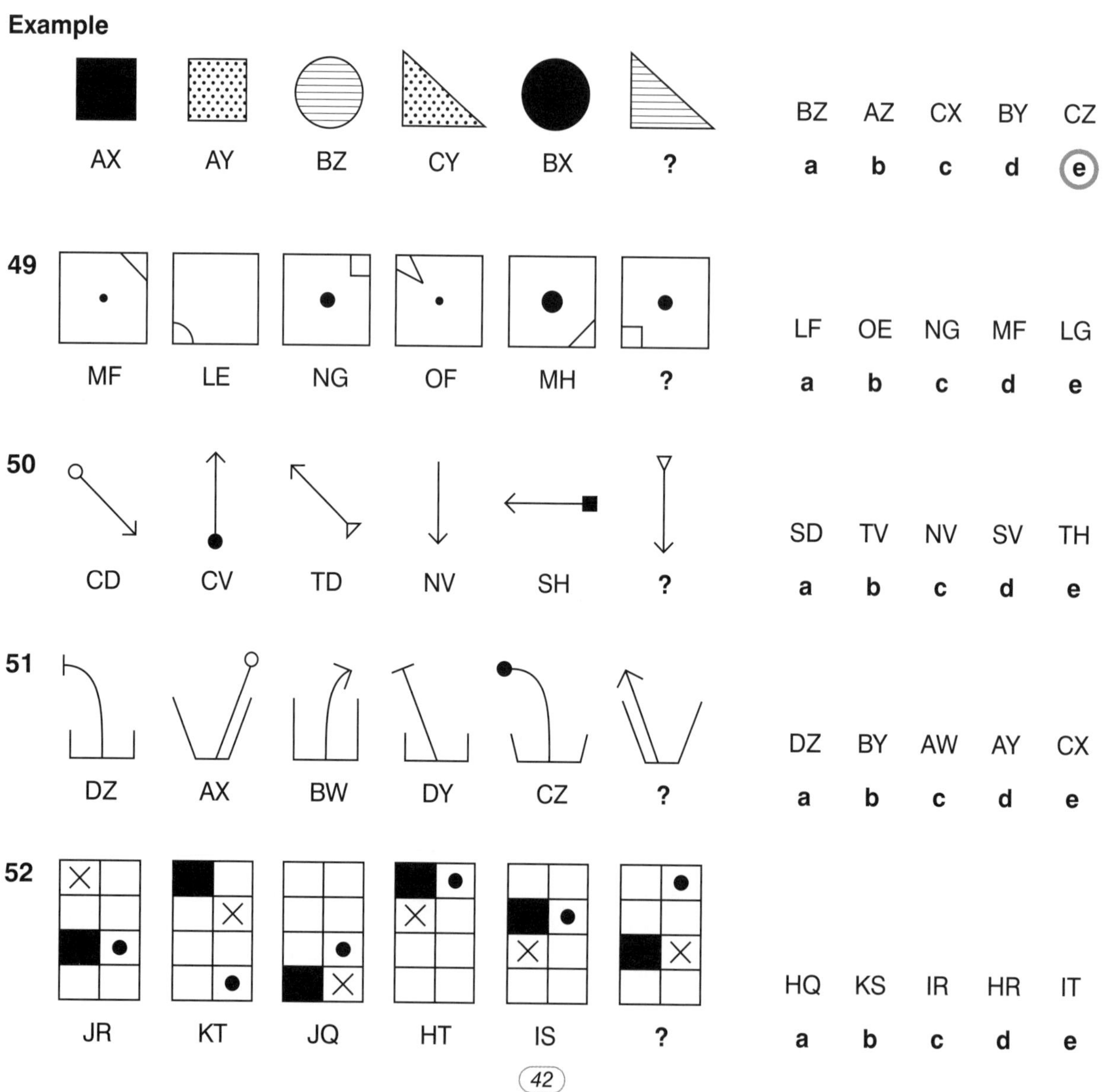

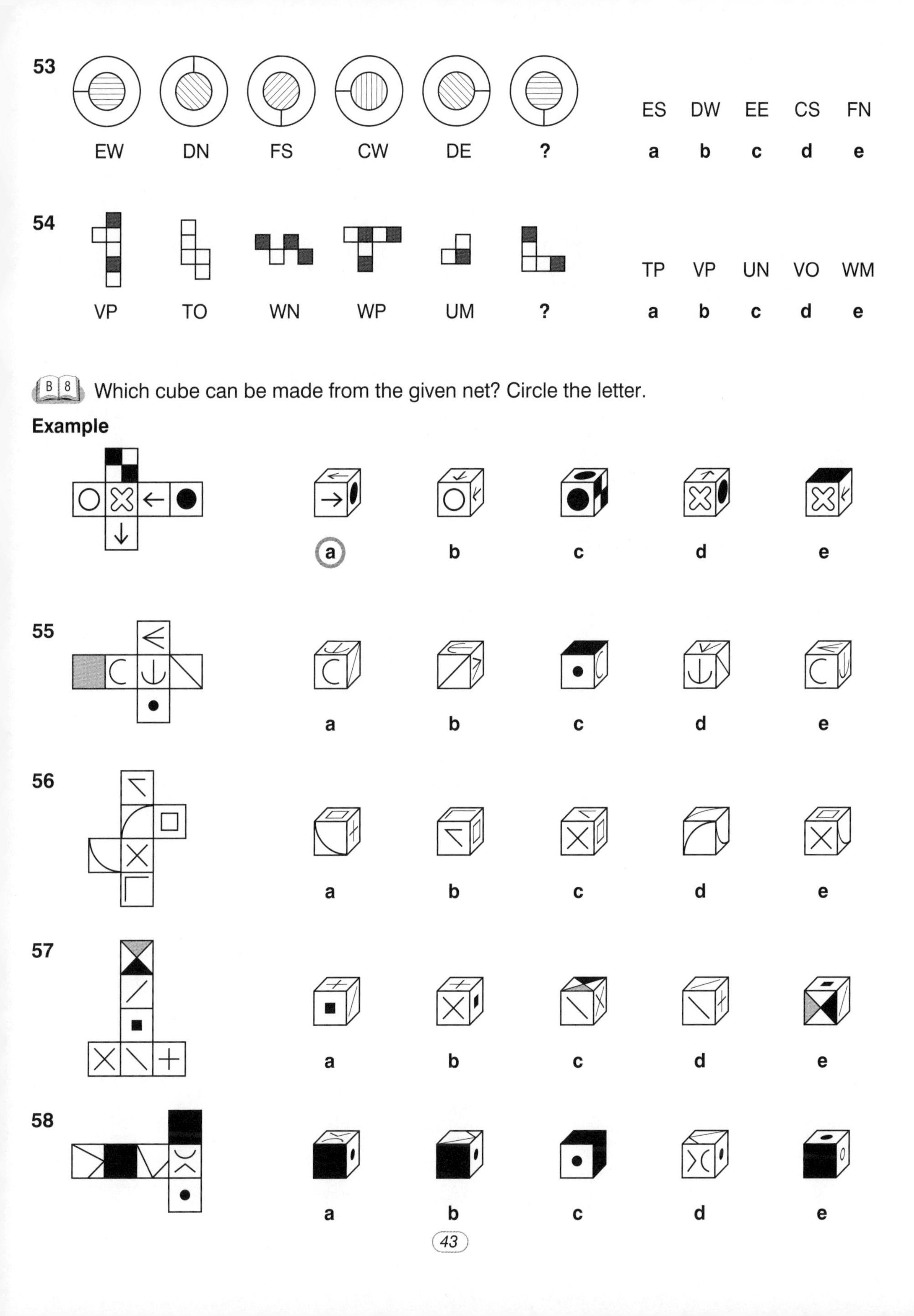
53
EW
DN
FS
CW
DE
?
ES DW EE CS FN
a b c d e
54
VP
TO
WN
WP
UM
?
TP VP UN VO WM
a b c d e
B 8
Which cube can be made from the given net? Circle the letter.
Example
a b c d e
55
a b c d e
56
a b c d e
57
a b c d e
58
a b c d e

59

60

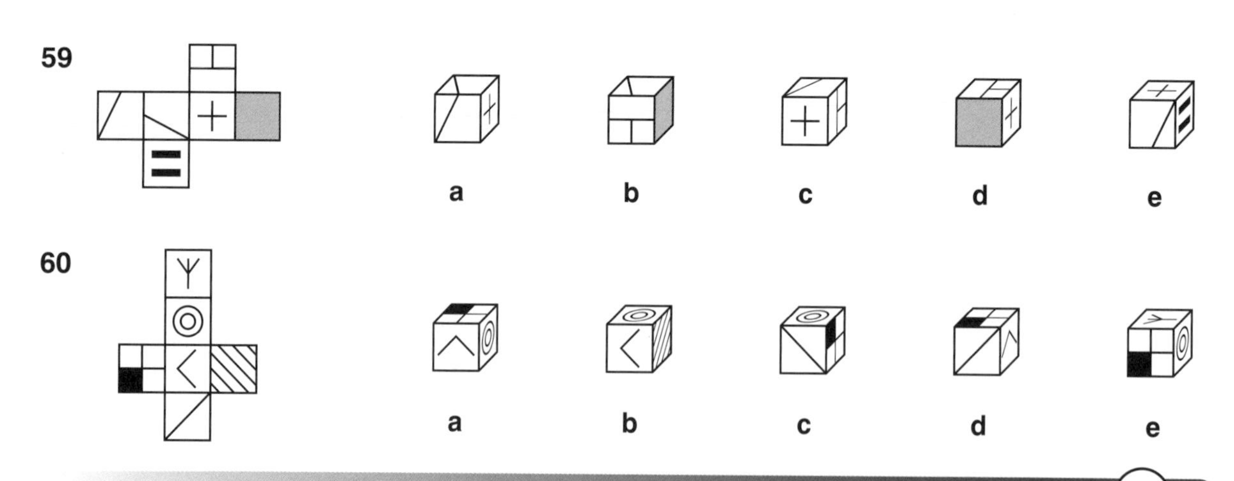

Now go to the Progress Chart to record your score!
Total
60

Paper 5

B 4 Which one comes next? Circle the letter.

Example

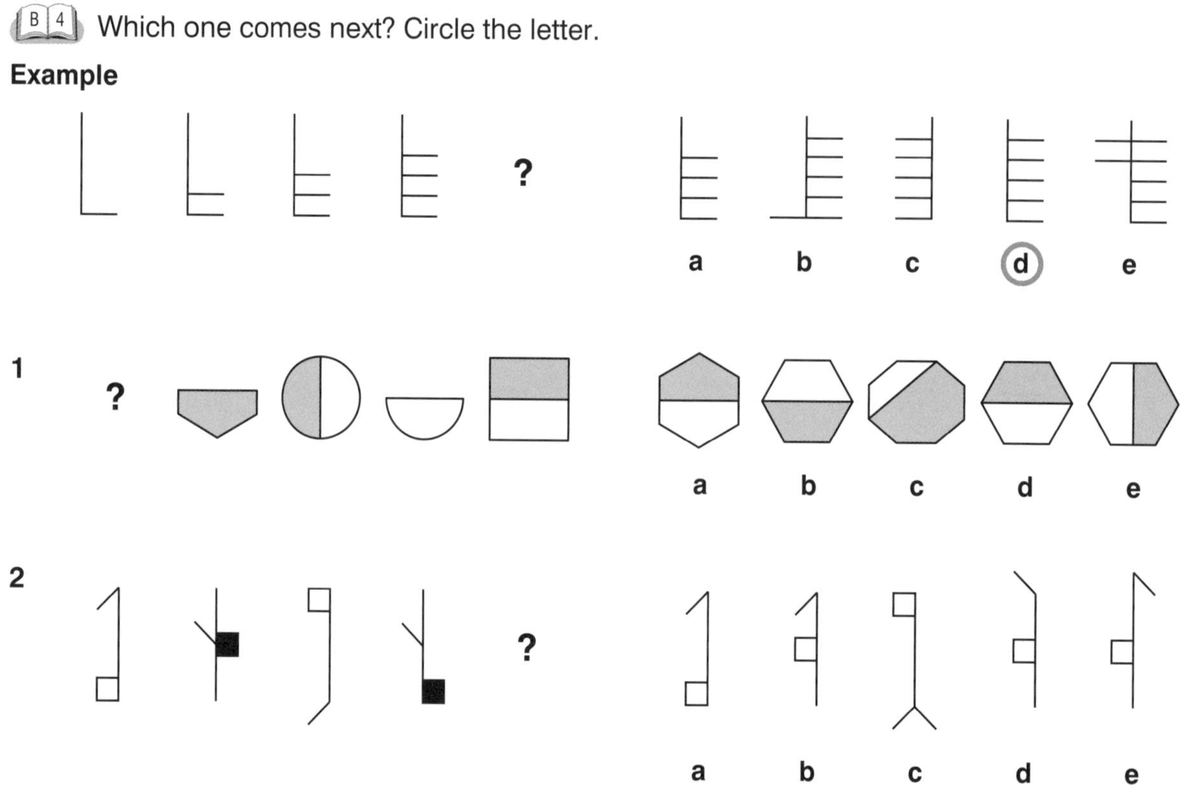

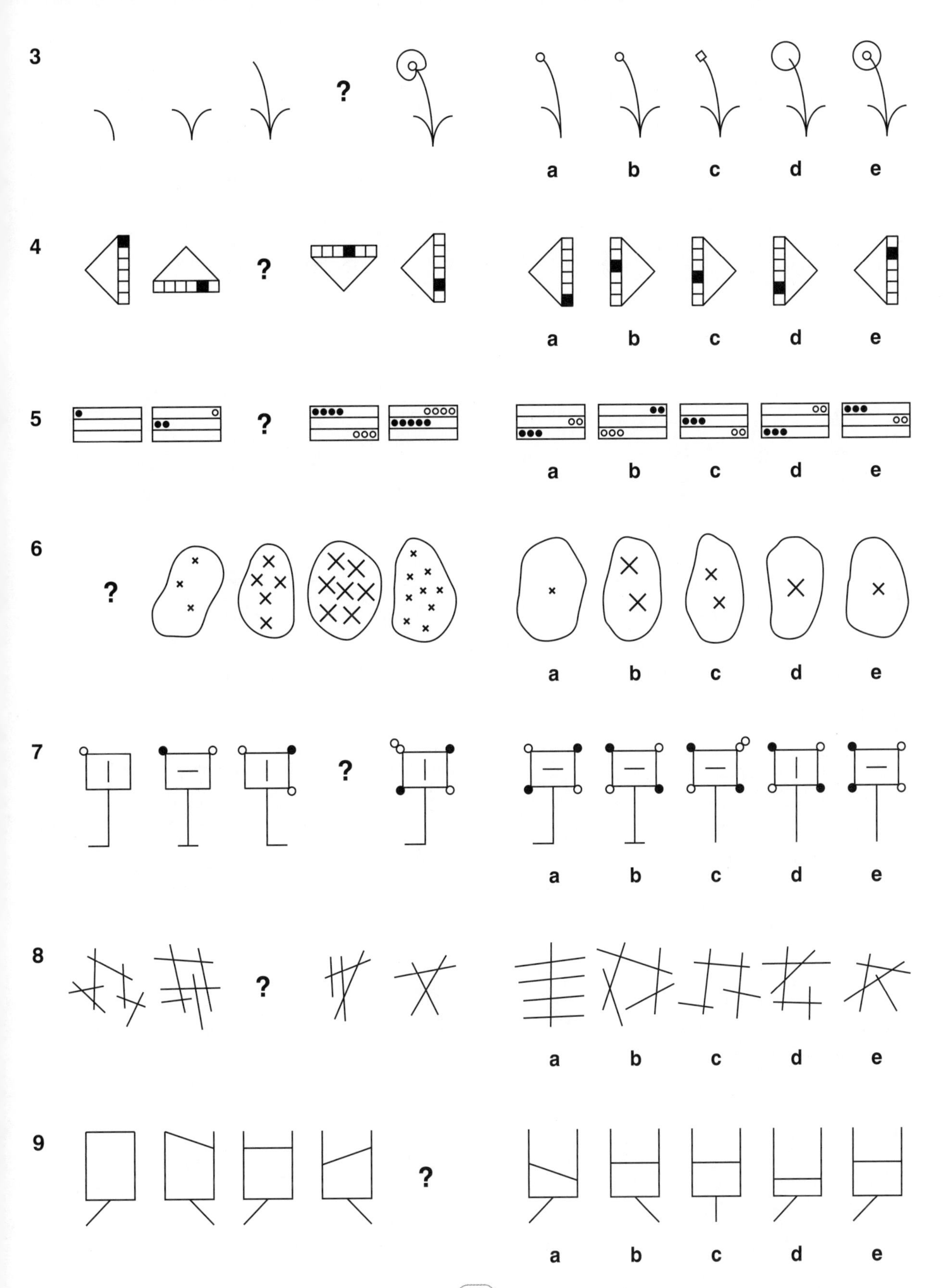
3
?
a
b
c
d
e
4
?
a
b
c
d
e
5
?
a
b
c
d
e
6
?
a
b
c
d
e
7
?
a
b
c
d
e
8
?
a
b
c
d
e
9
?
a
b
c
d
e

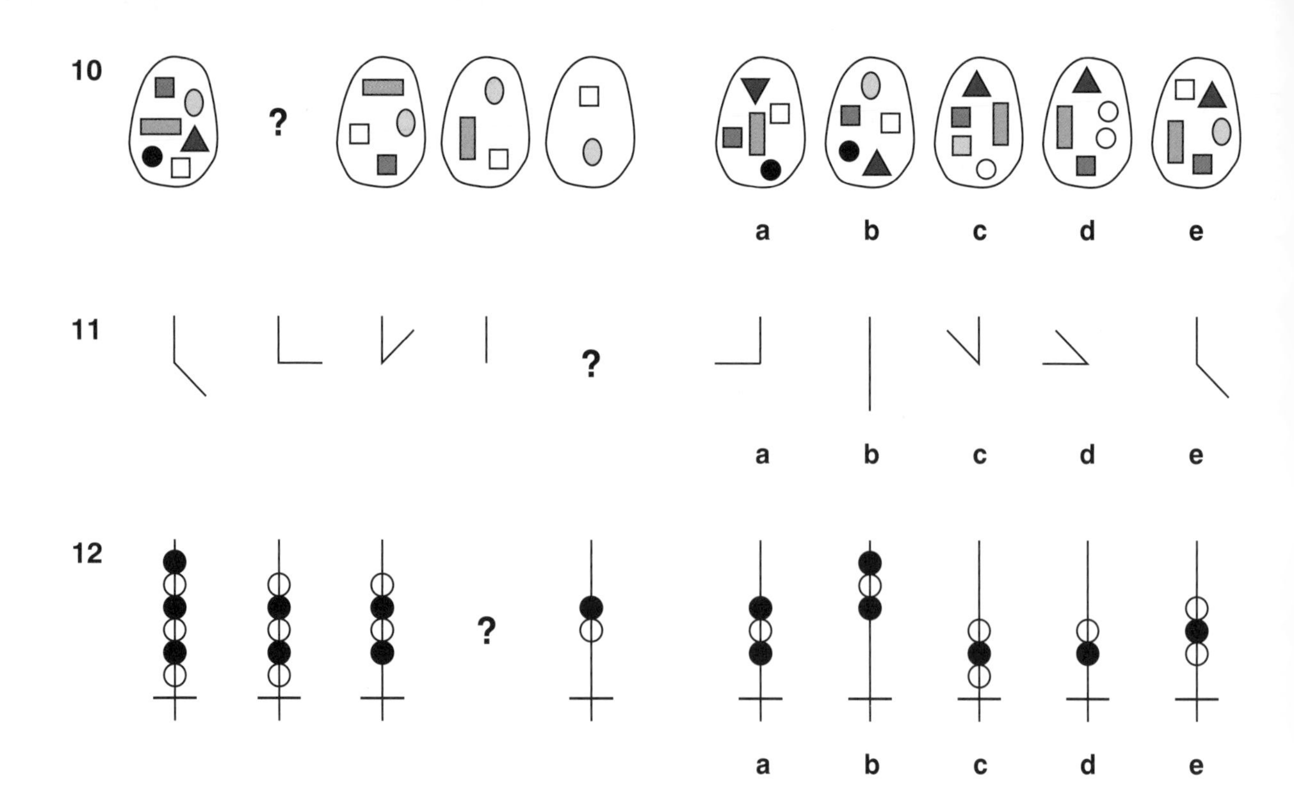

B 2 Which pattern on the right belongs in the group on the left? Circle the letter.

Example

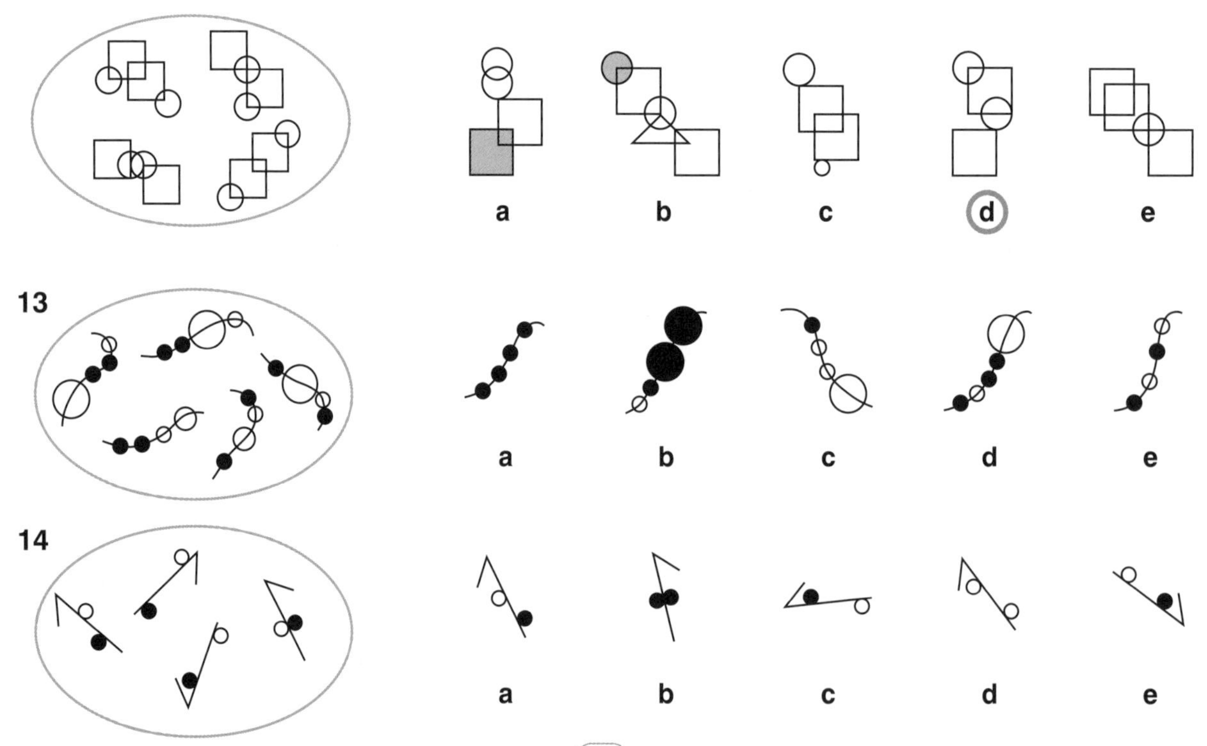

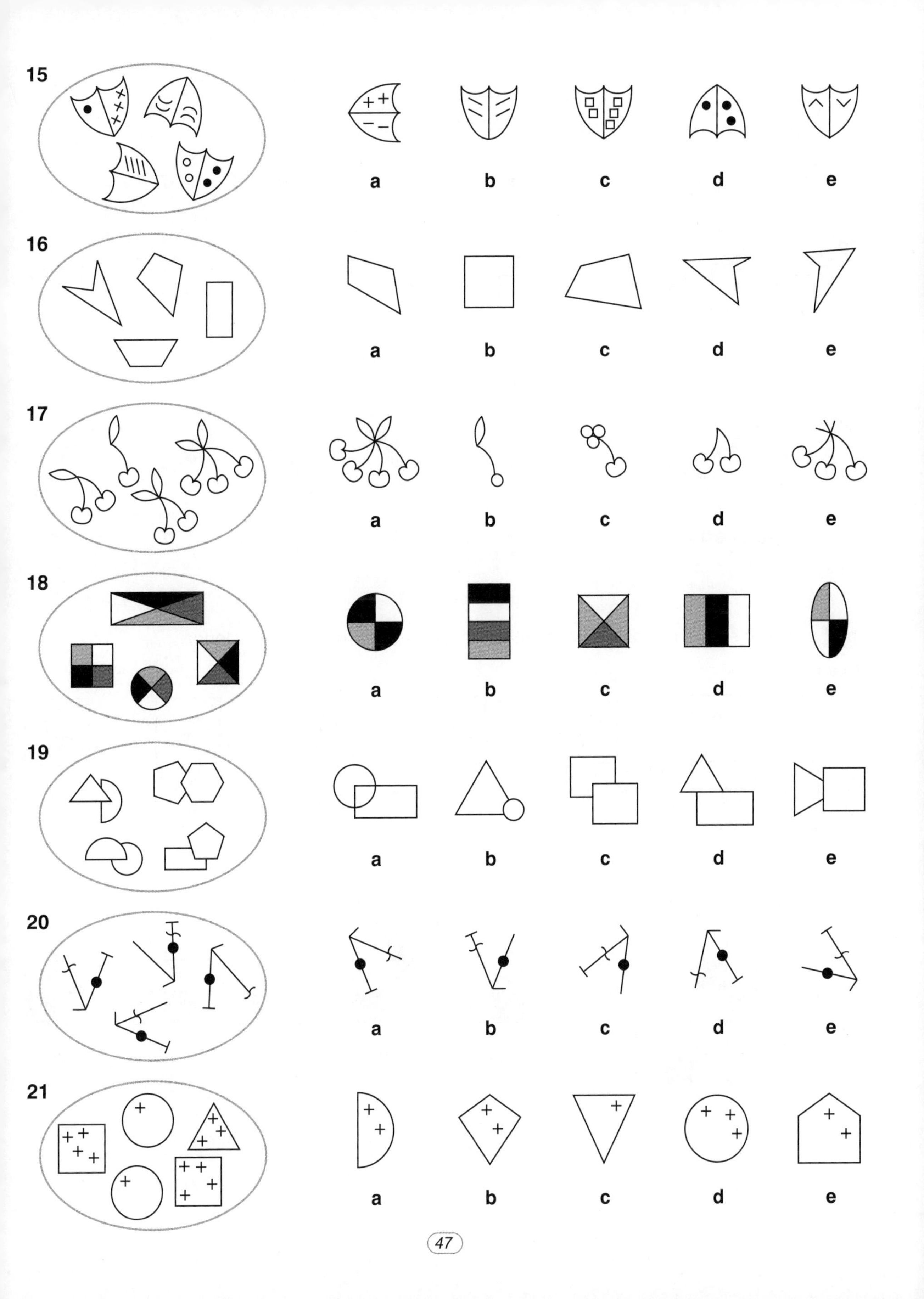
15
a
b
c
d
e
16
a
b
c
d
e
17
a
b
c
d
e
18
a
b
c
d
e
19
a
b
c
d
e
20
a
b
c
d
e
21
a
b
c
d
e

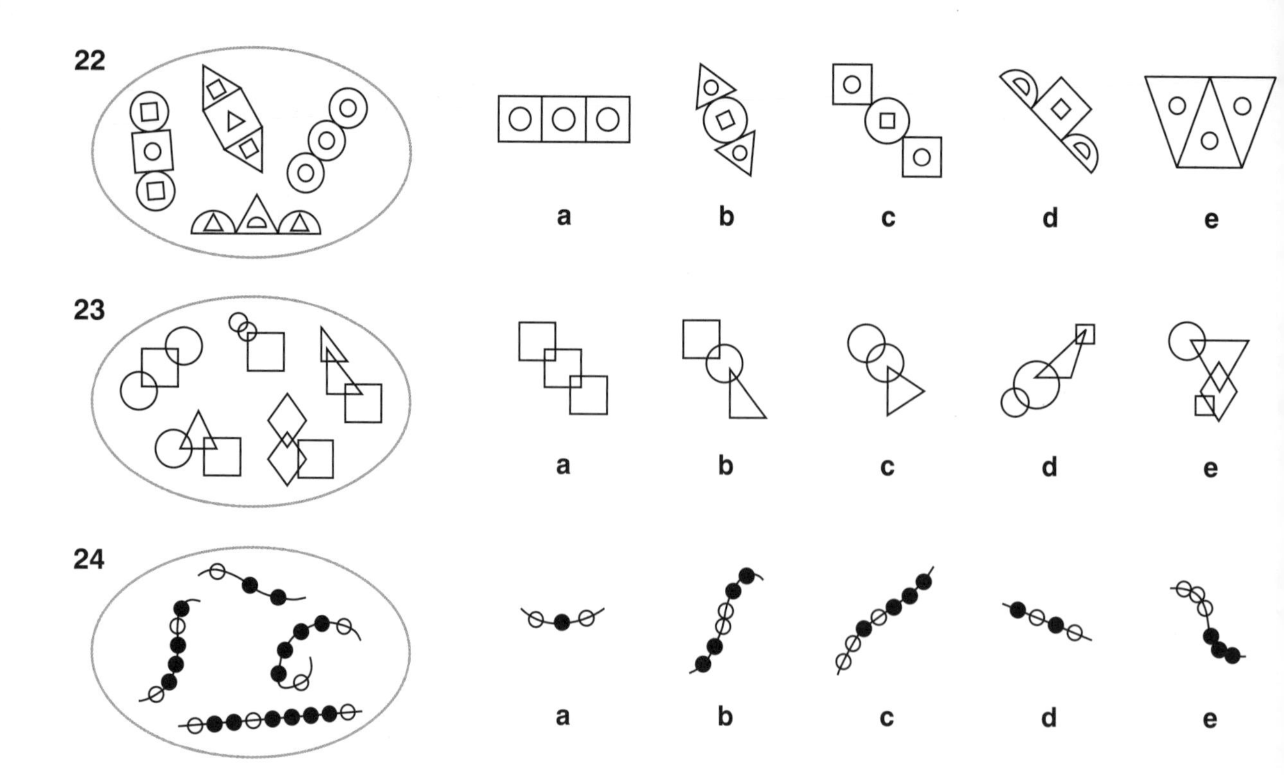

B 6 Which shape or pattern completes the larger square? Circle the letter.

Example

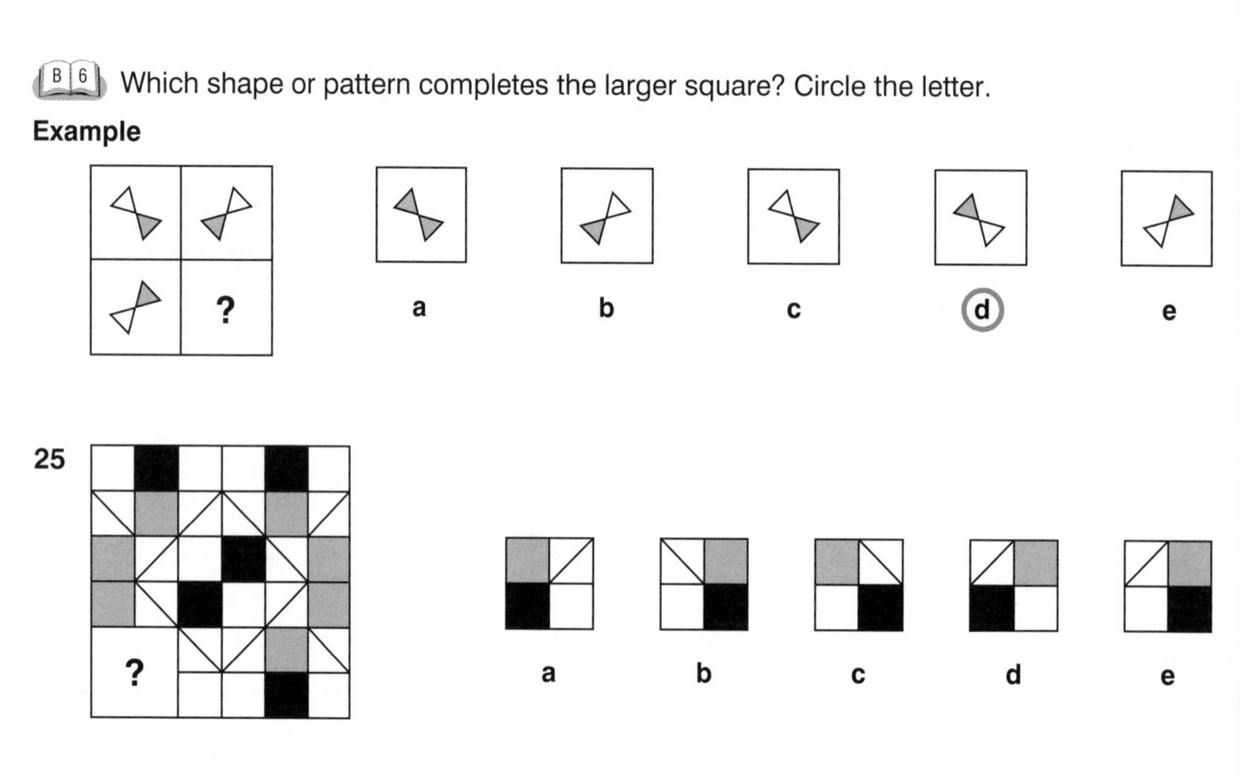

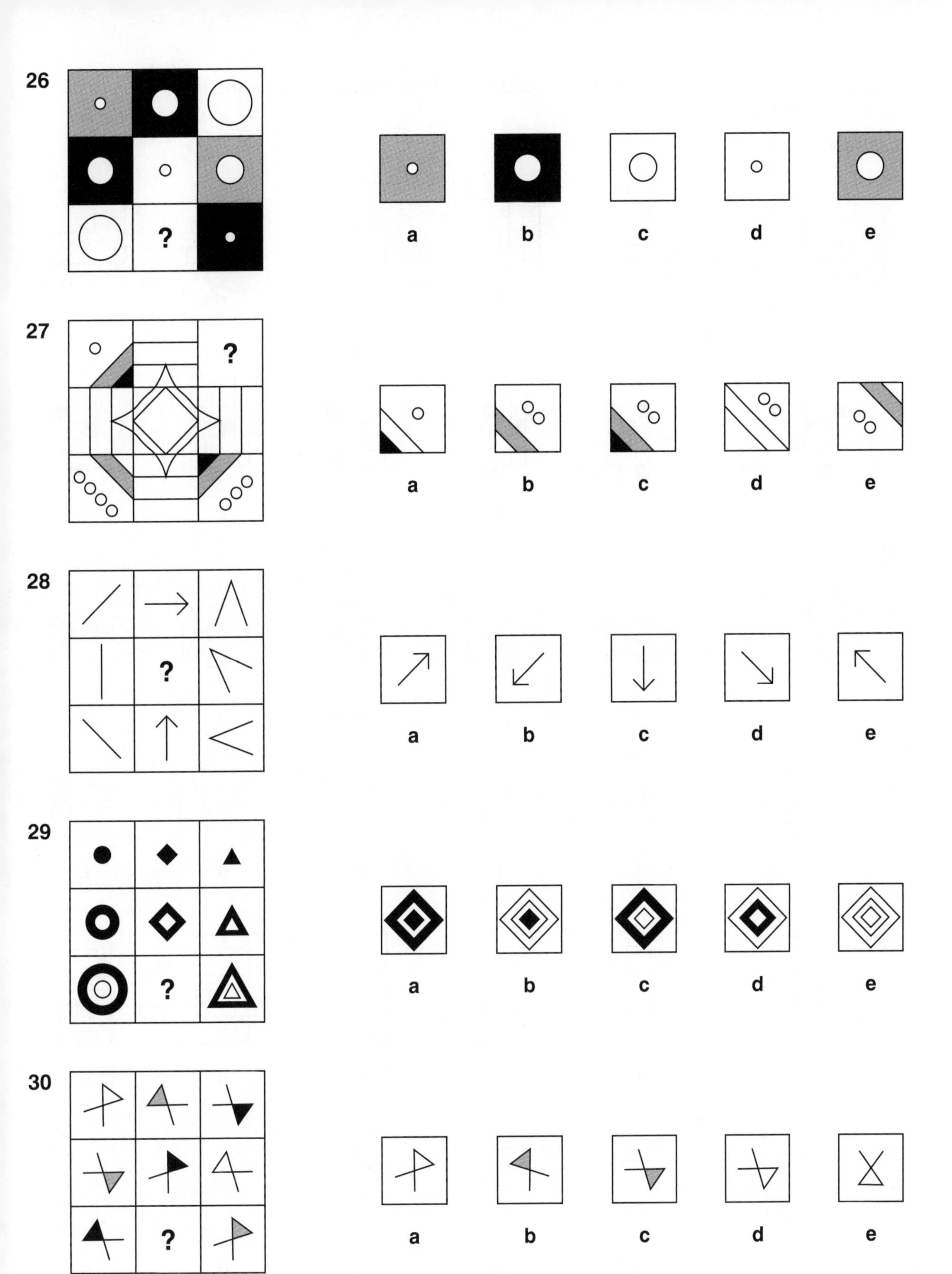
26
?
a
b
c
d
e
27
?
a
b
c
d
e
28
?
a
b
c
d
e
29
?
a
b
c
d
e
30
?
a
b
c
d
e

B7 Which shape on the right is the reflection of the shape given on the left? Circle the letter.

Example

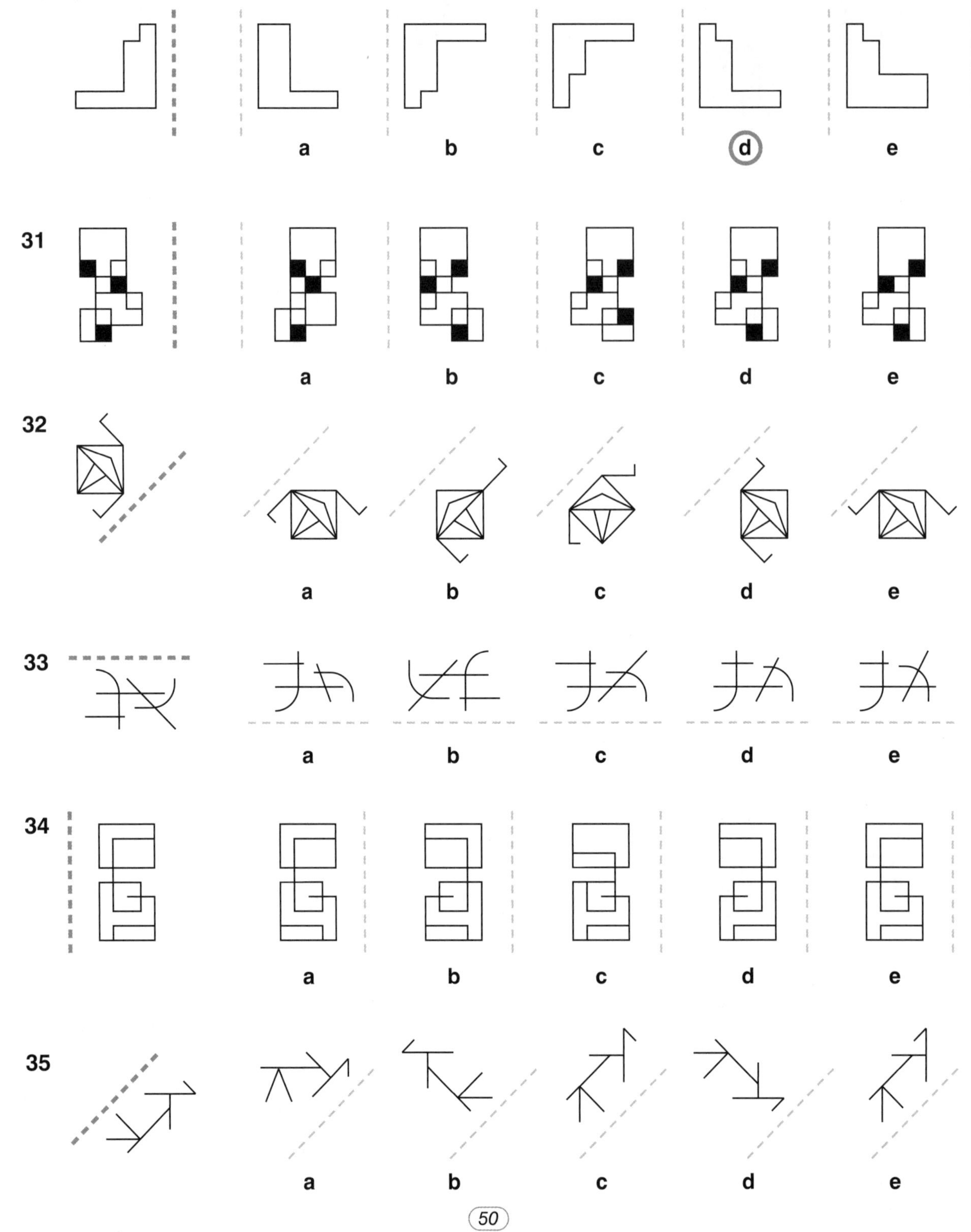

36 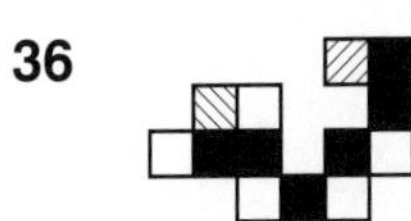 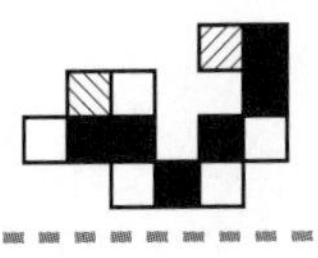

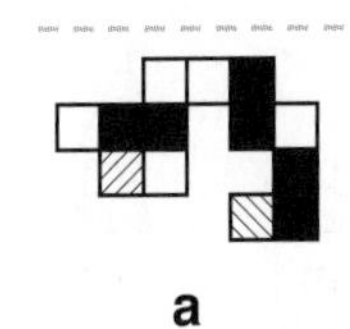 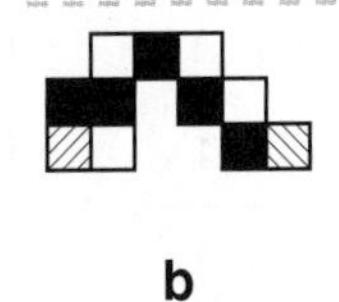 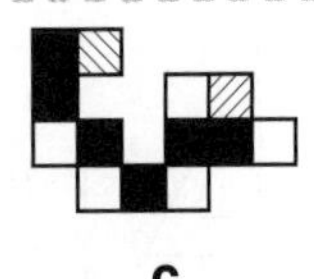  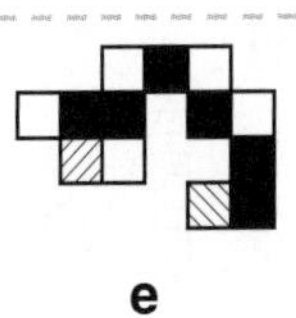

a b c d e

B3 Which shape or pattern on the right completes the second pair in the same way as the first pair? Circle the letter.

Example

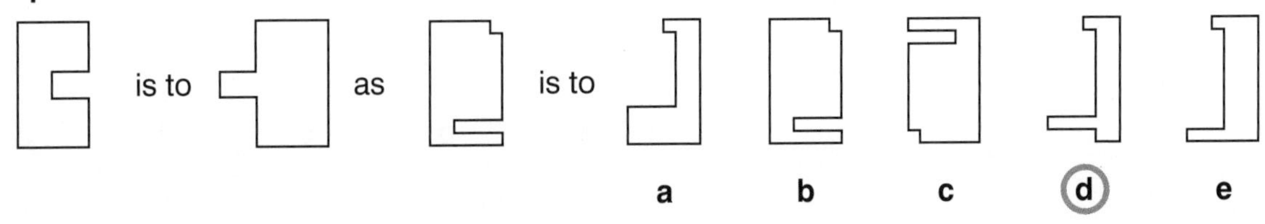

a b c (d) e

37

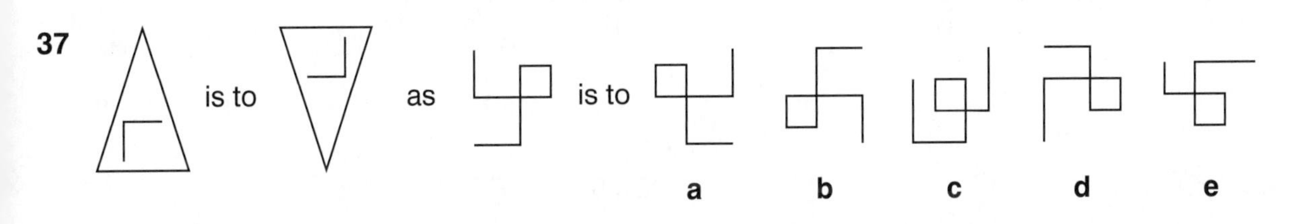

38

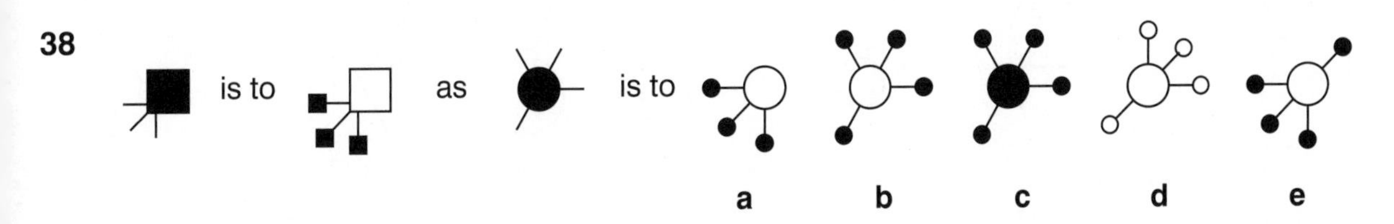

39

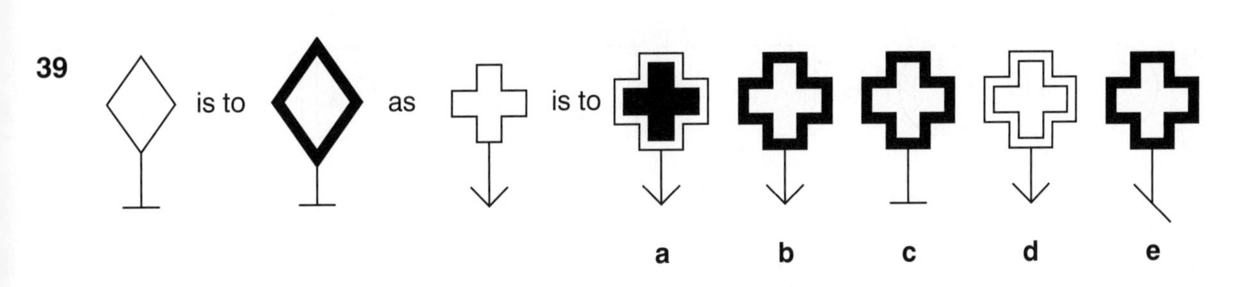

40

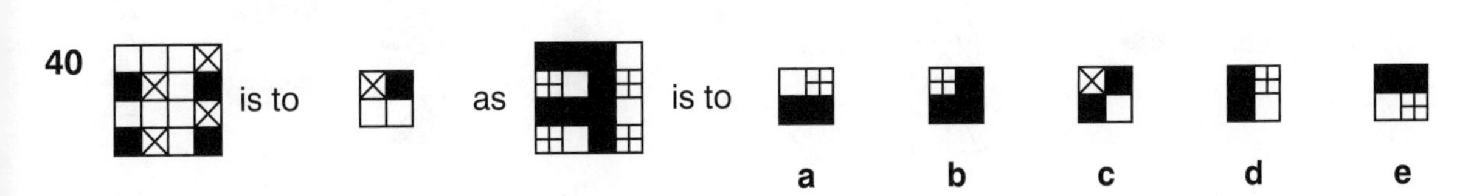

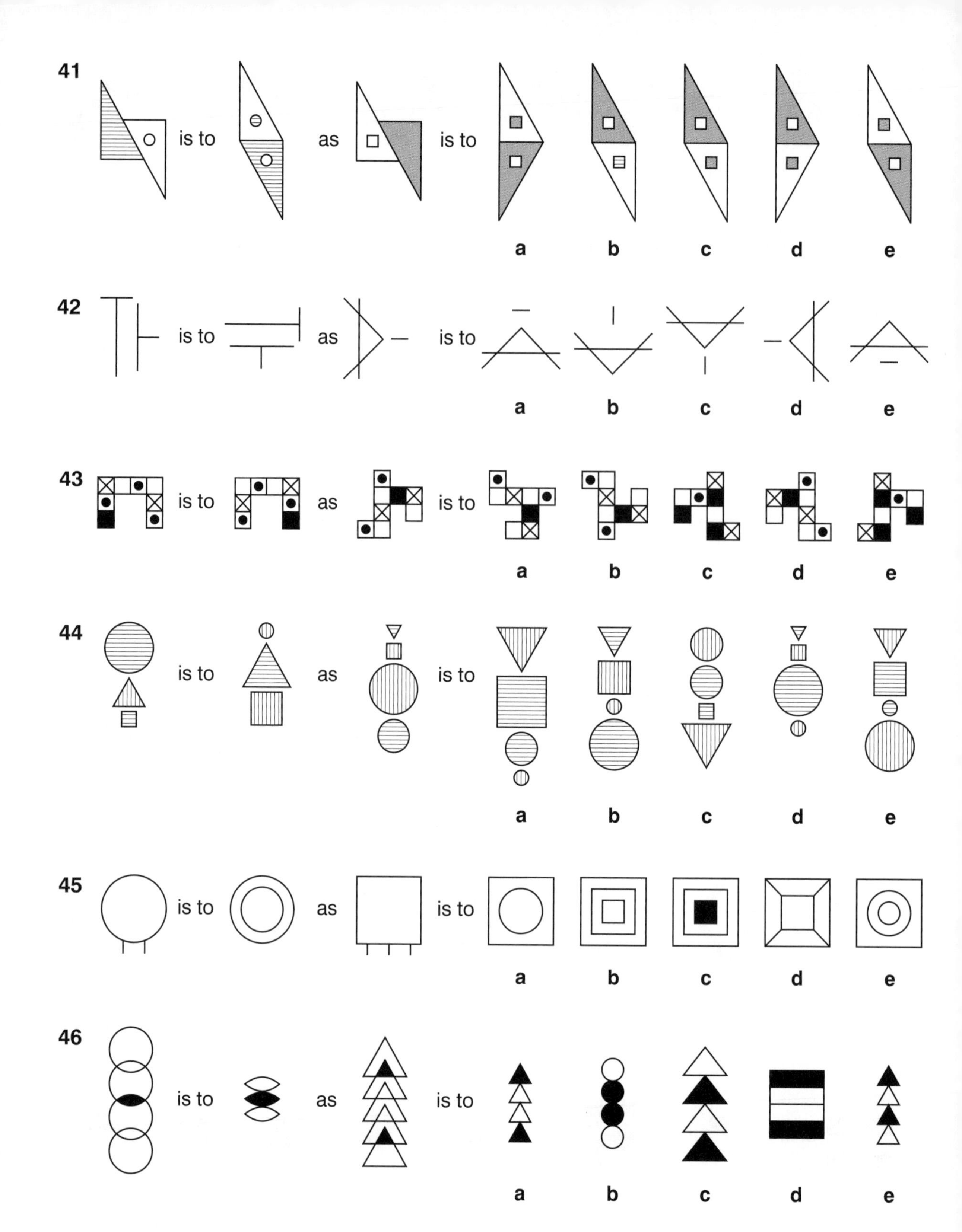
41
is to
as
is to
a
b
c
d
e
42
is to
as
is to
a
b
c
d
e
43
is to
as
is to
a
b
c
d
e
44
is to
as
is to
a
b
c
d
e
45
is to
as
is to
a
b
c
d
e
46
is to
as
is to
a
b
c
d
e

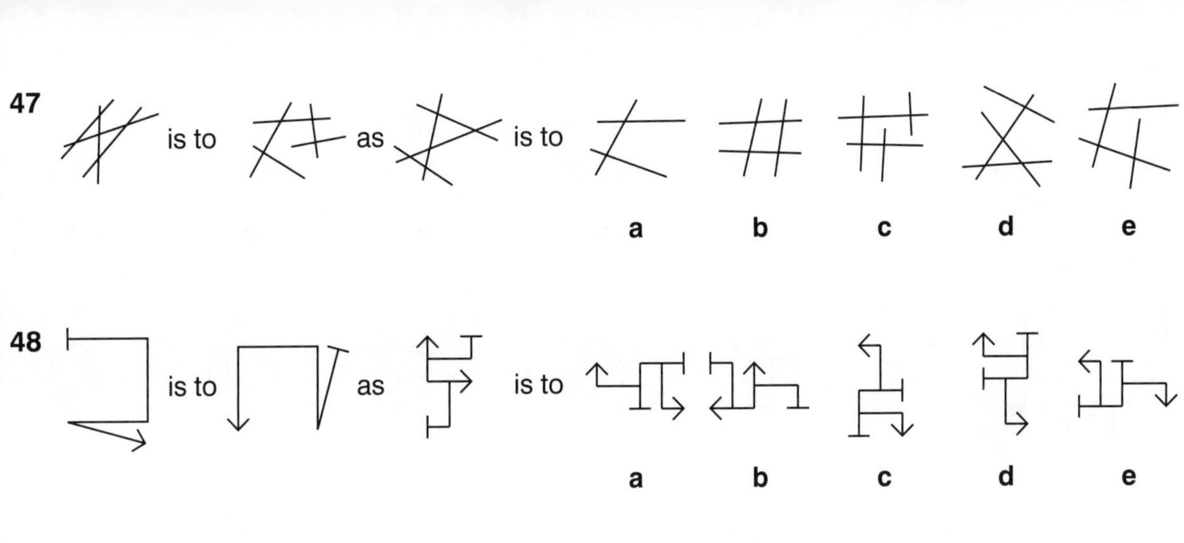

Which cube cannot be made from the given net? Circle the letter.

Example

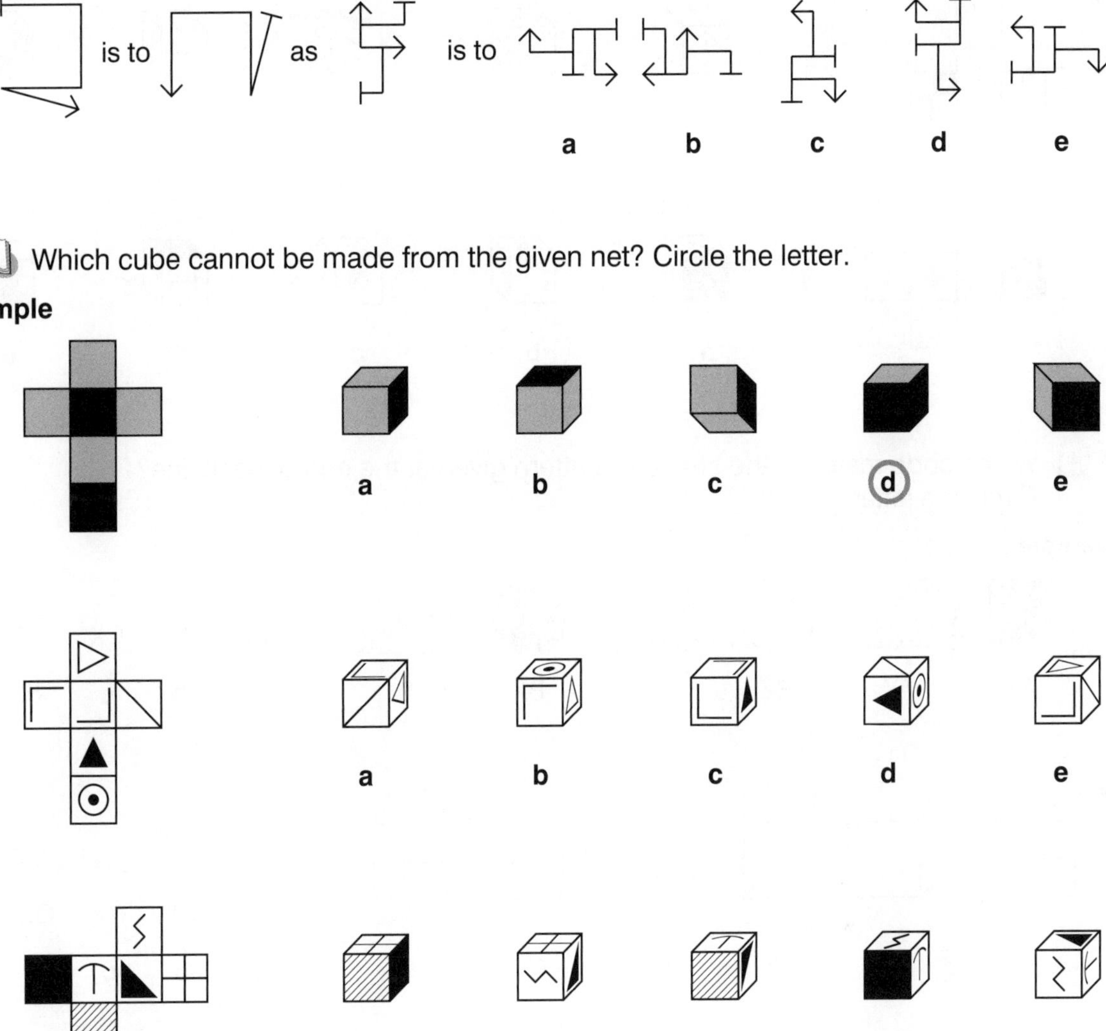

a b c d e

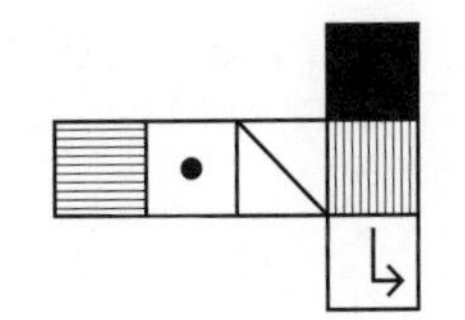

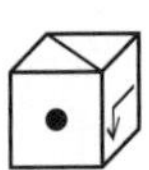

a b c d e

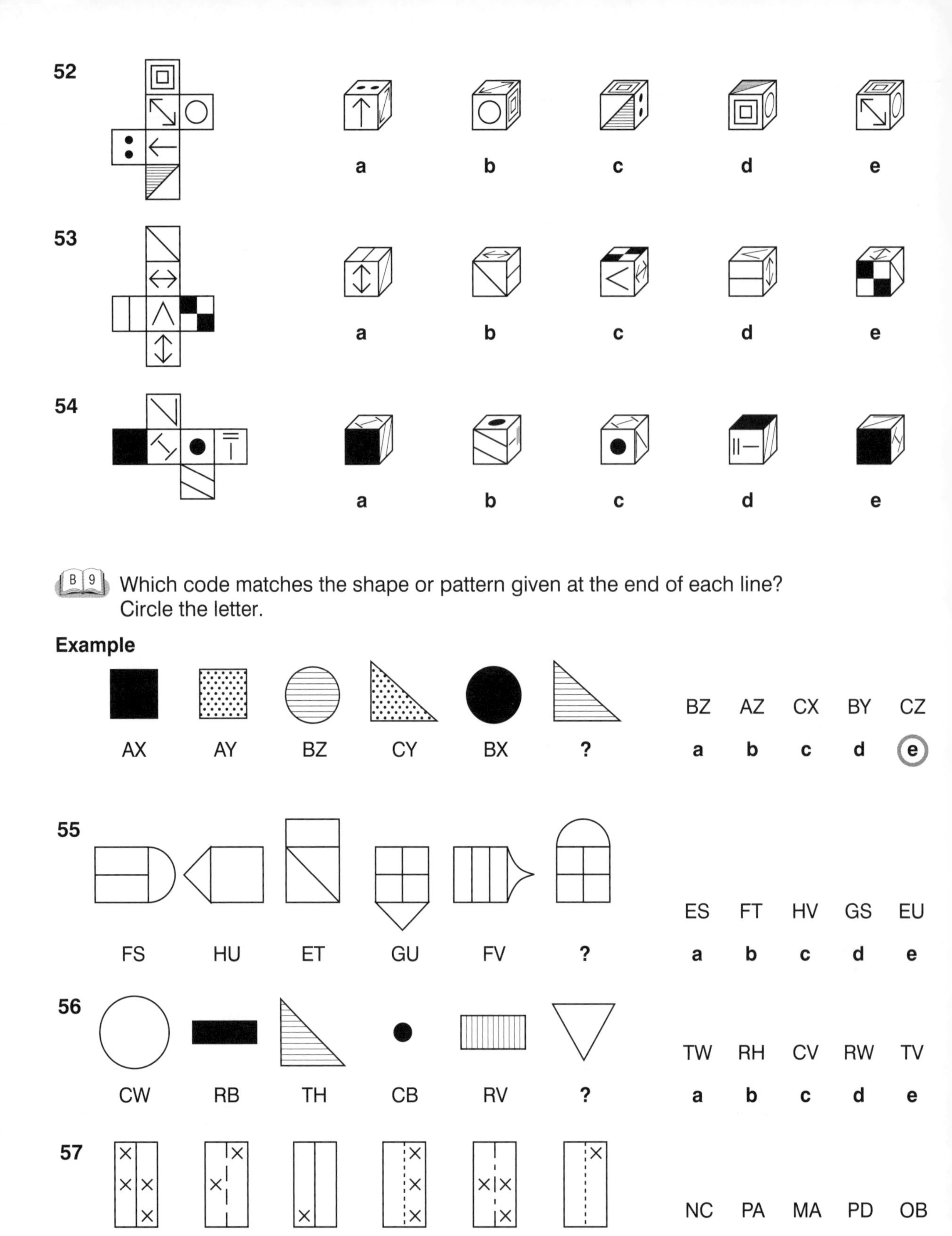
52
a
b
c
d
e
53
a
b
c
d
e
54
a
b
c
d
e
B 9
Which code matches the shape or pattern given at the end of each line?
Circle the letter.
Example
AX
AY
BZ
CY
BX
?
BZ AZ CX BY CZ
a b c d e
55
FS
HU
ET
GU
FV
?
ES FT HV GS EU
a b c d e
56
CW
RB
TH
CB
RV
?
TW RH CV RW TV
a b c d e
57
MD
OC
PD
NA
NB
?
NC PA MA PD OB
a b c d e

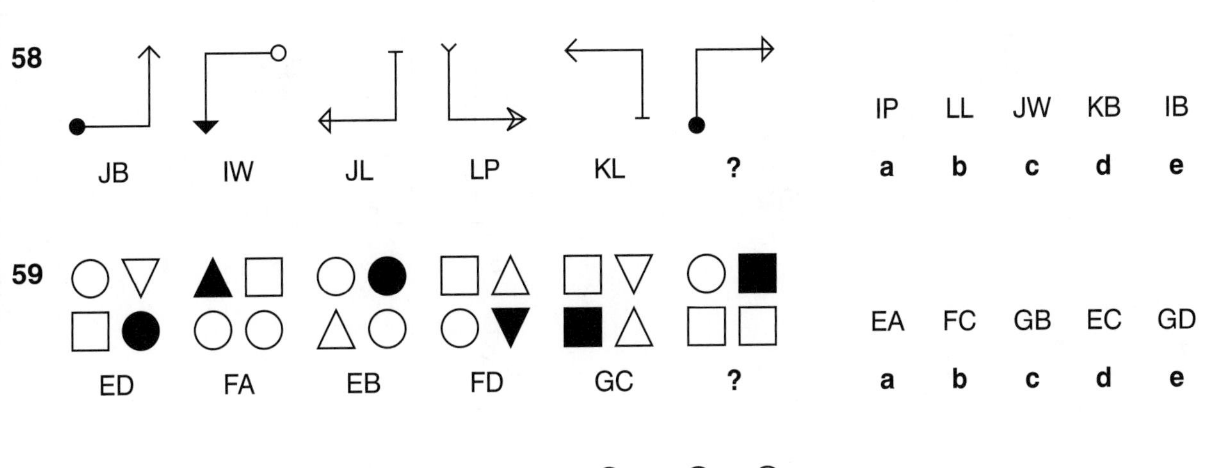

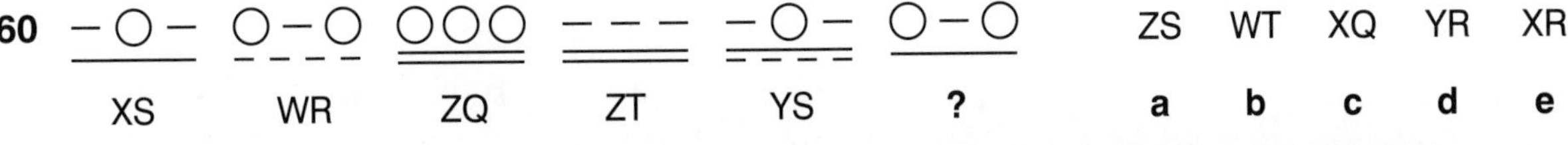

Now go to the Progress Chart to record your score! **Total** / 60

Paper 6

B4 Which one comes next? Circle the letter.

Example

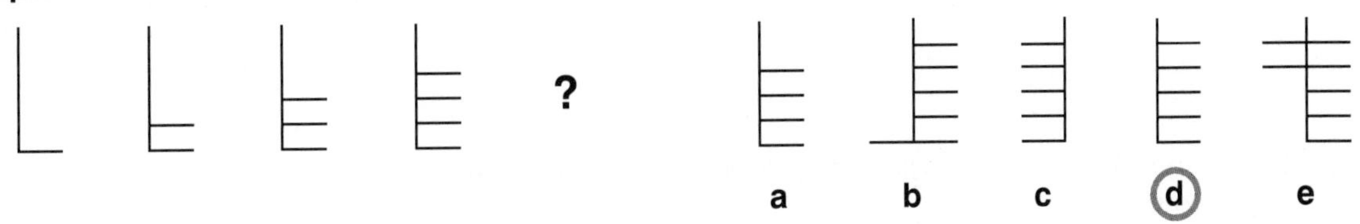

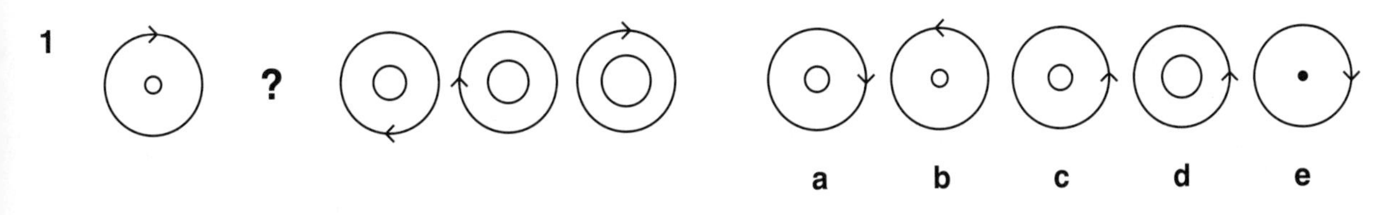

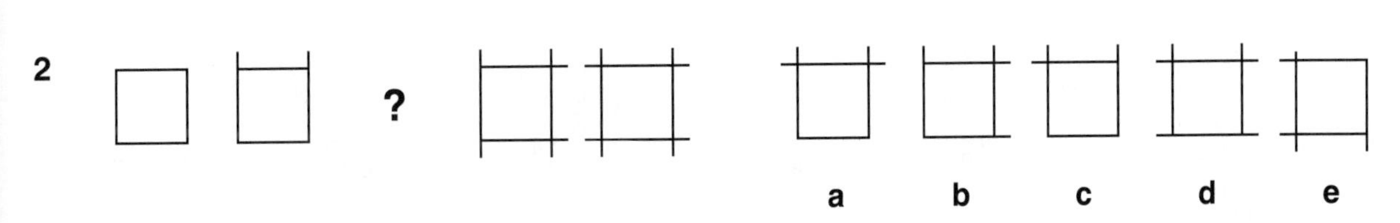

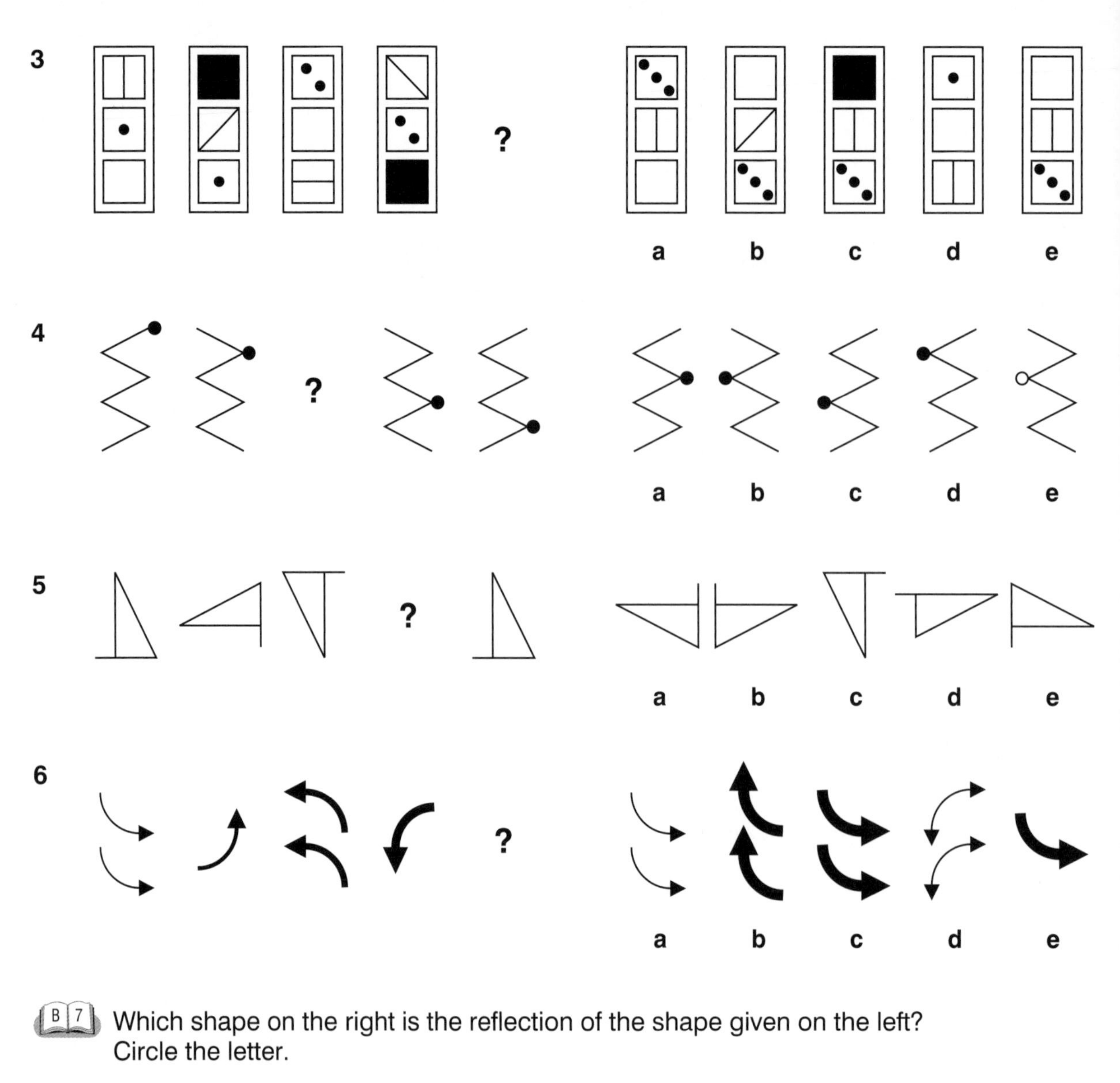

B 7 Which shape on the right is the reflection of the shape given on the left?
Circle the letter.

Example

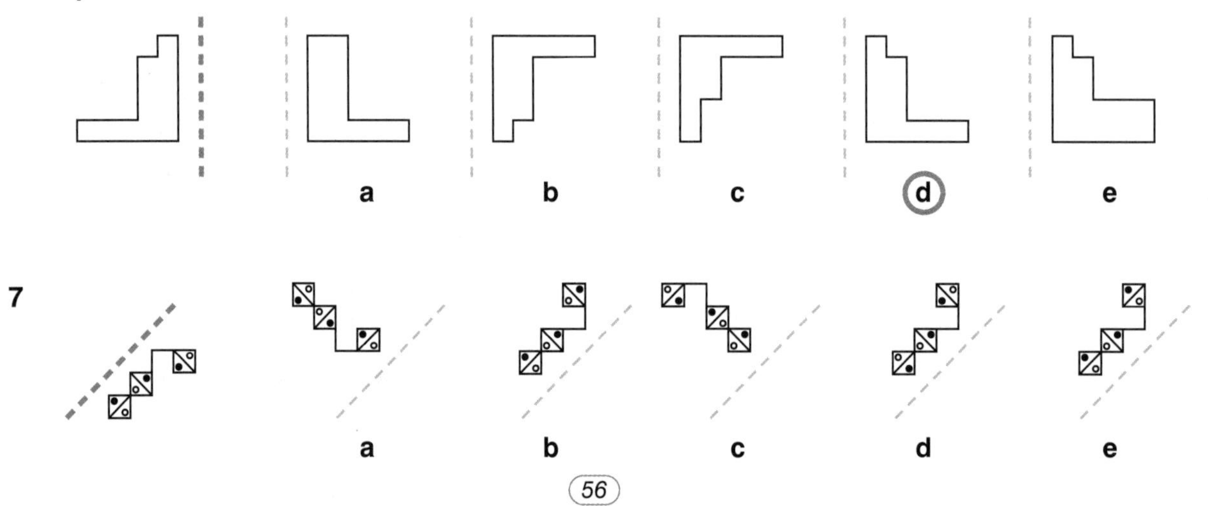

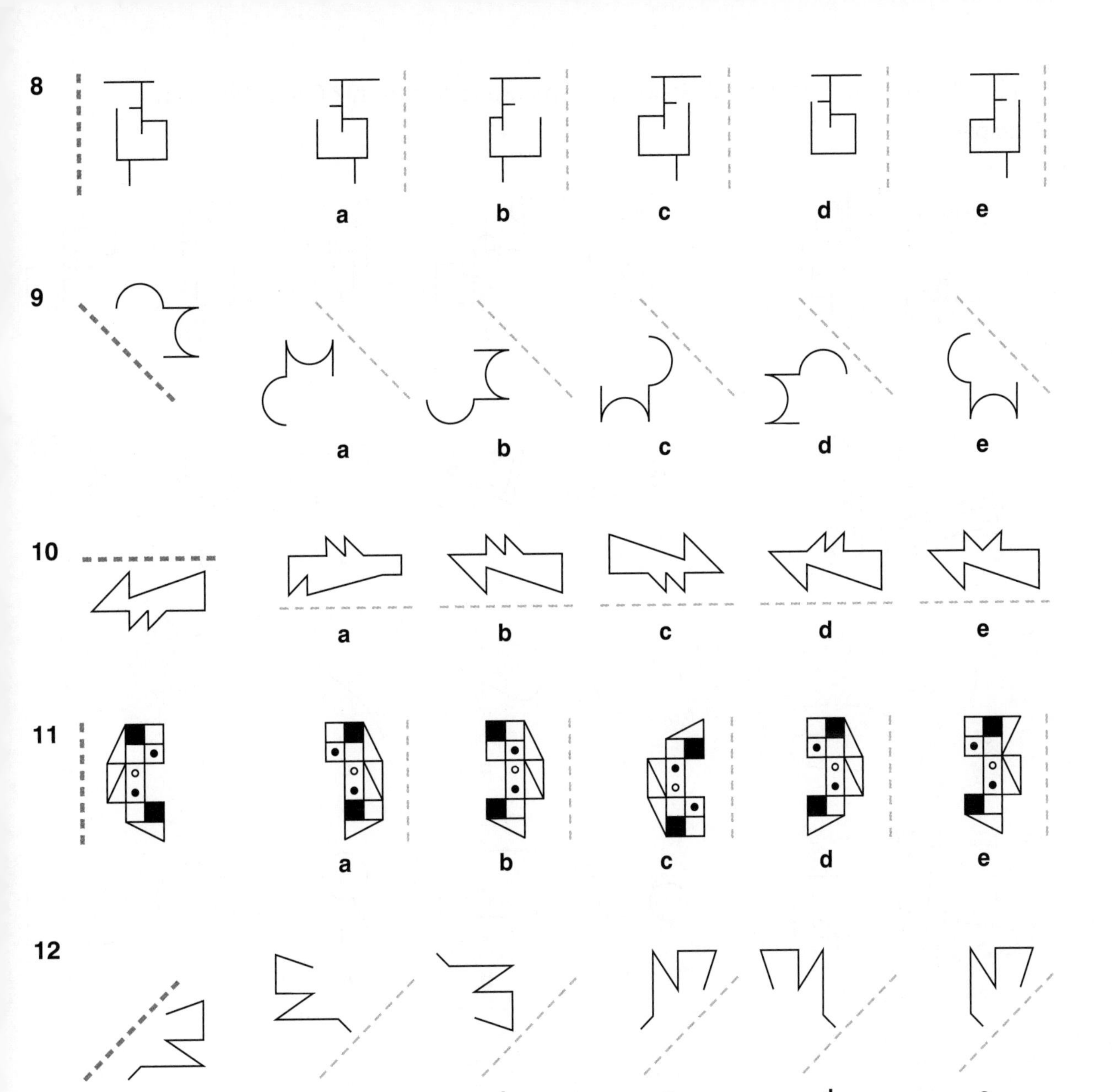
8
a
b
c
d
e
9
a
b
c
d
e
10
a
b
c
d
e
11
a
b
c
d
e
12
a
b
c
d
e

B 2 Which pattern on the right belongs in the group on the left? Circle the letter.

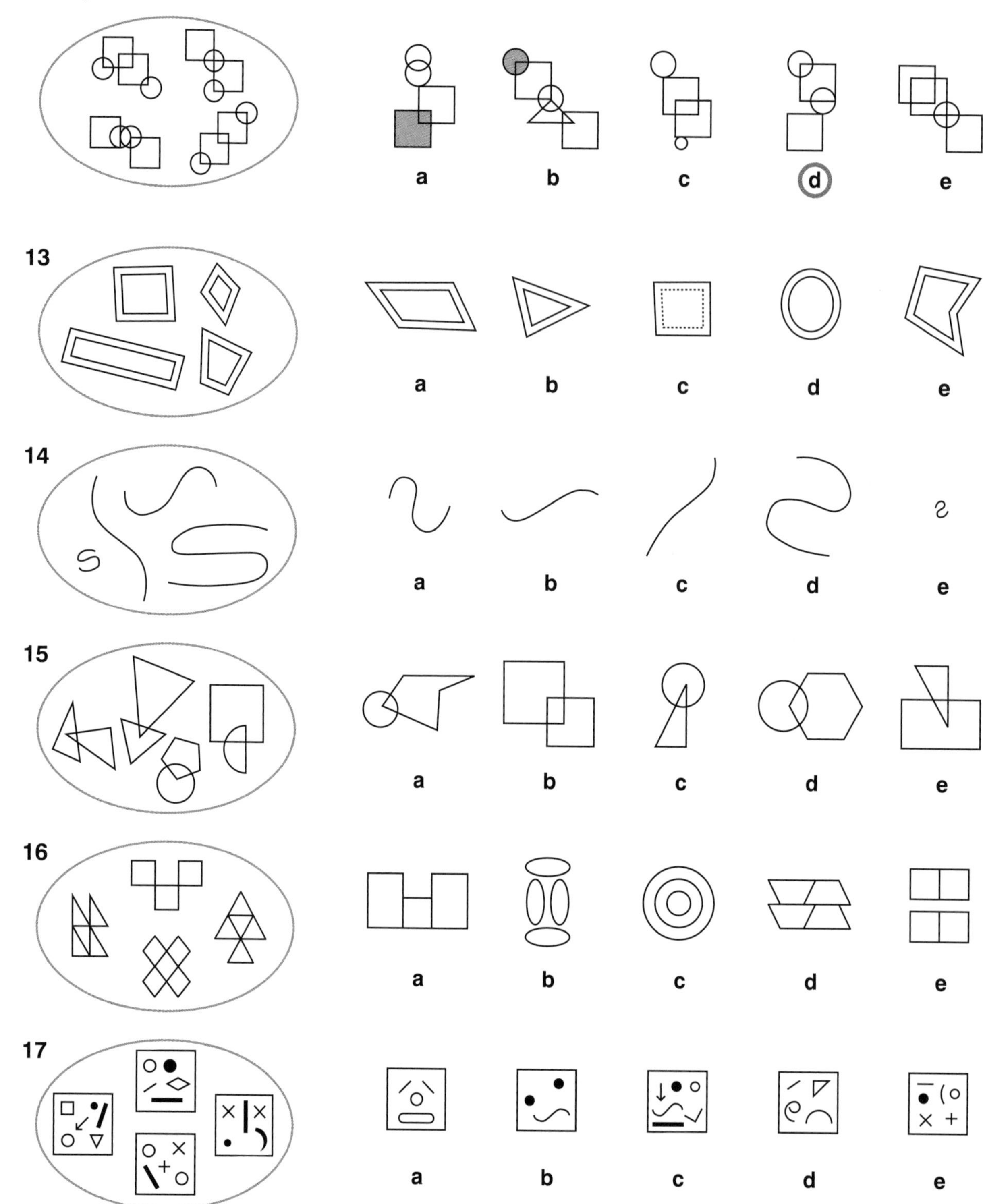

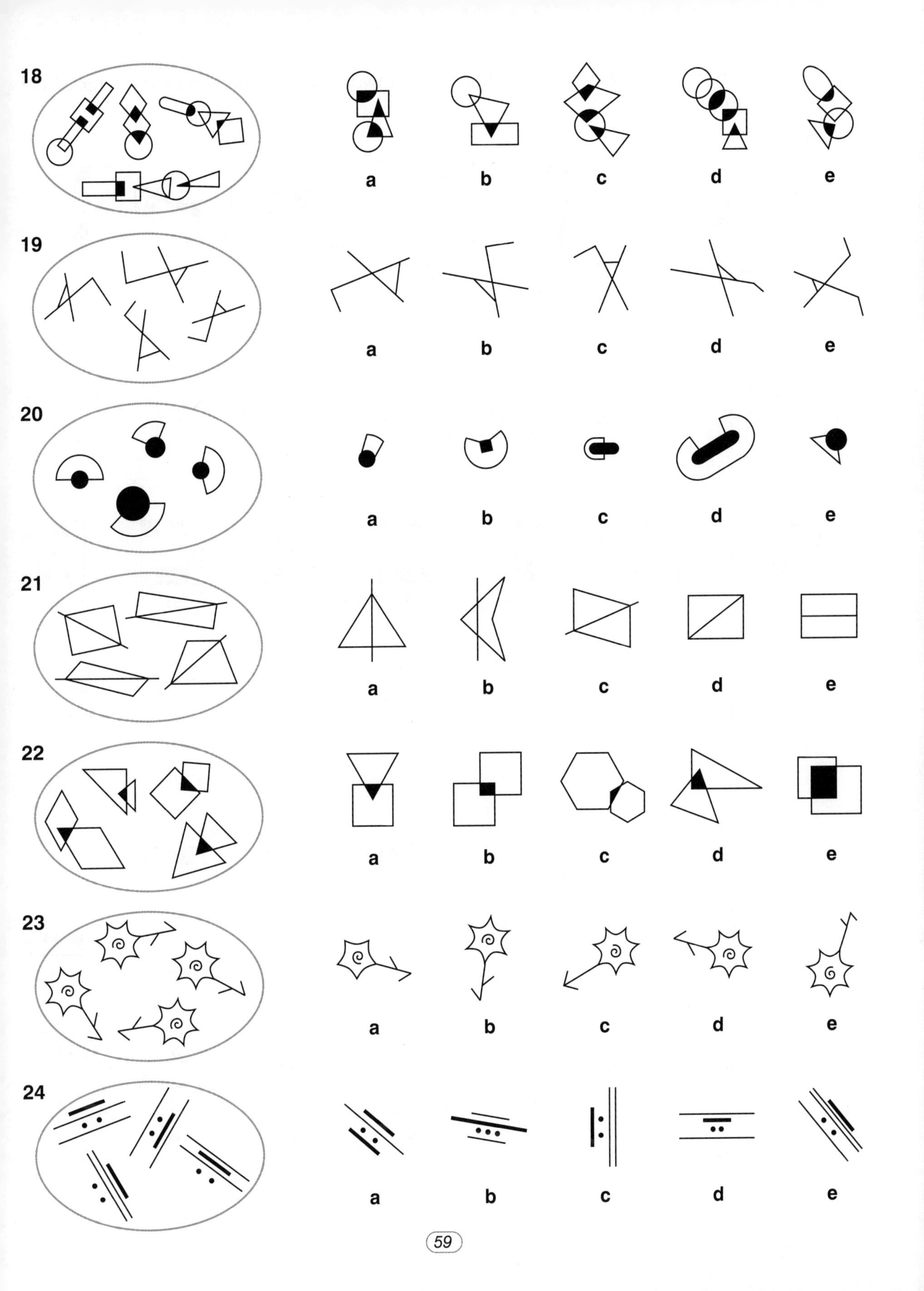
18
a
b
c
d
e
19
a
b
c
d
e
20
a
b
c
d
e
21
a
b
c
d
e
22
a
b
c
d
e
23
a
b
c
d
e
24
a
b
c
d
e

B 10 Which shape or pattern is made when the first two shapes or patterns are put together? Circle the letter.

Example

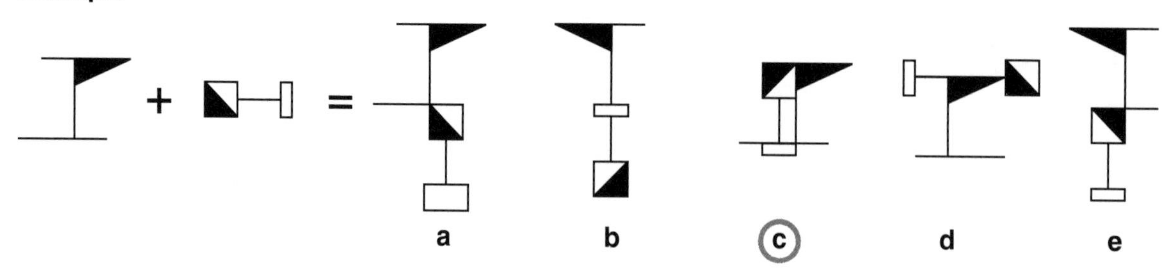

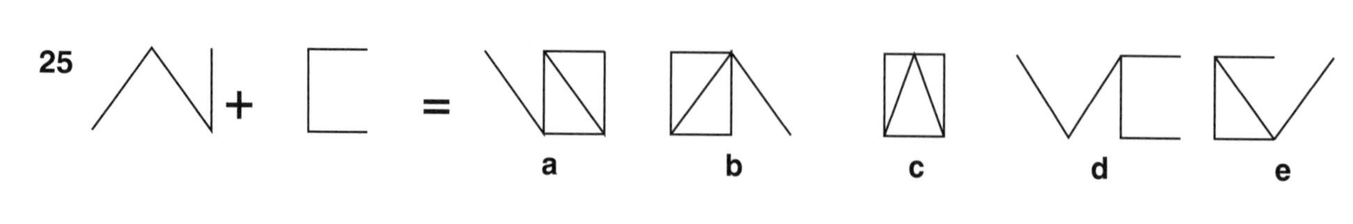

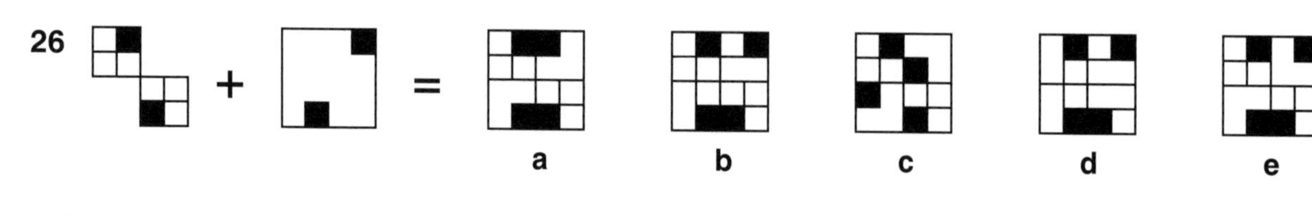

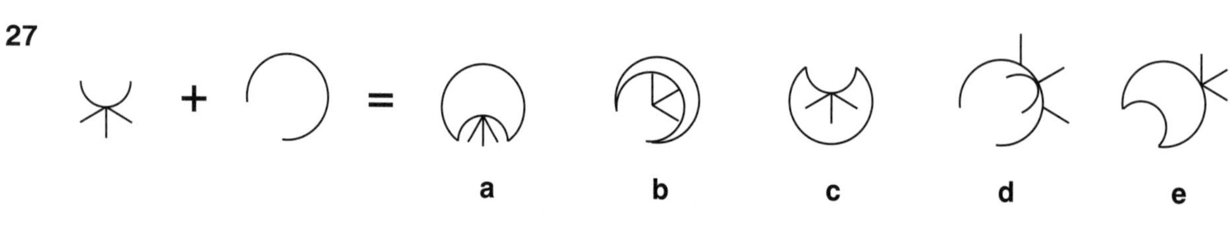

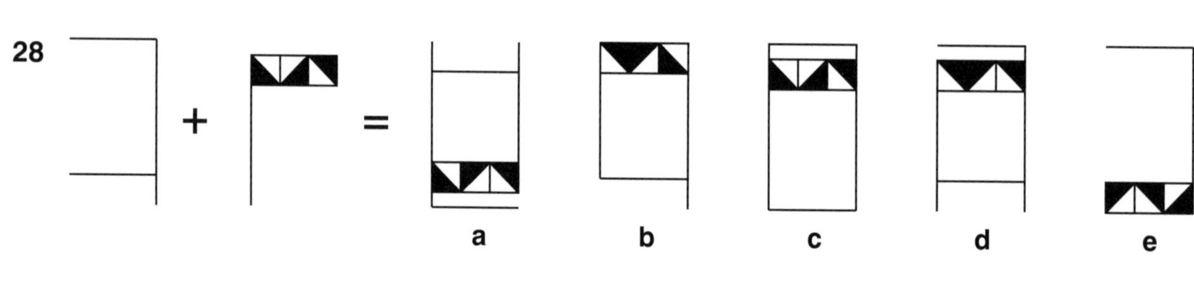

29 + =

a b c d e

30

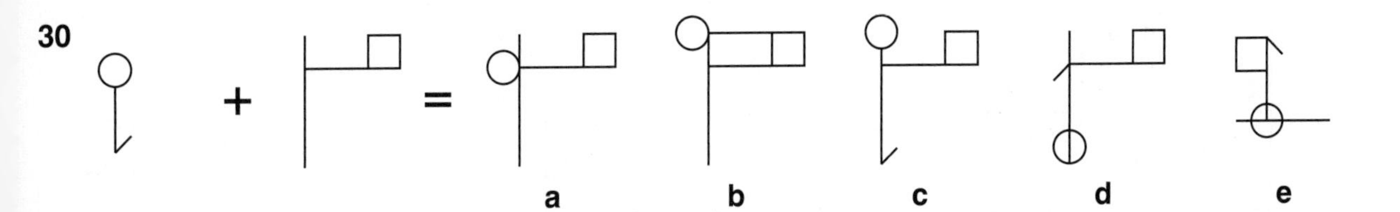

a b c d e

Which shape or pattern completes the larger square? Circle the letter.

Example

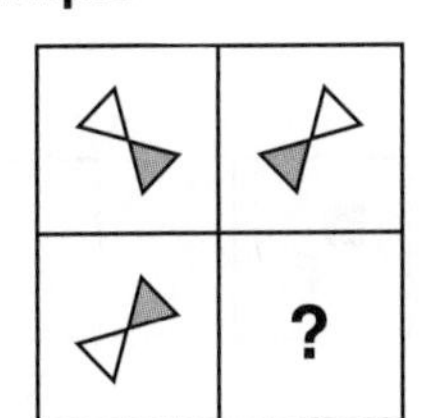

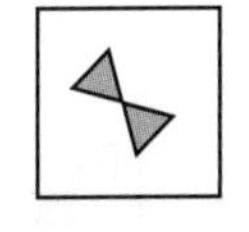 a

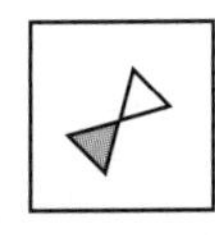 b

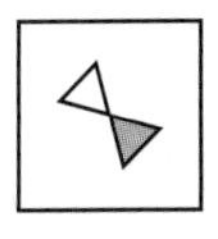 c

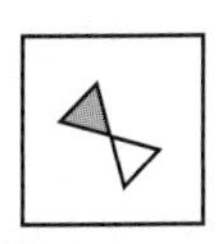 (d)

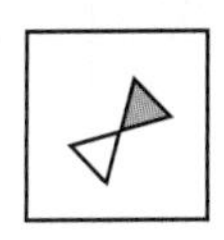 e

31

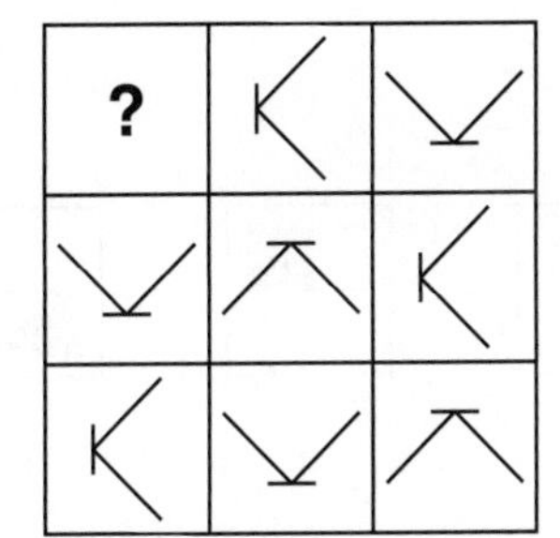

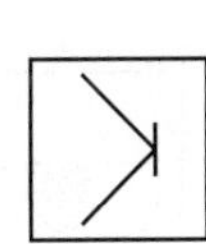 a

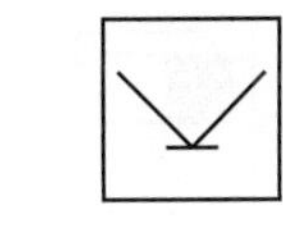 b

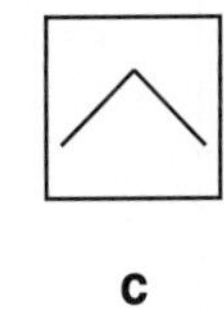 c

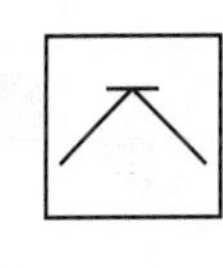 d

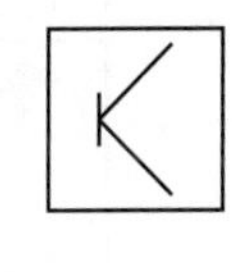 e

32

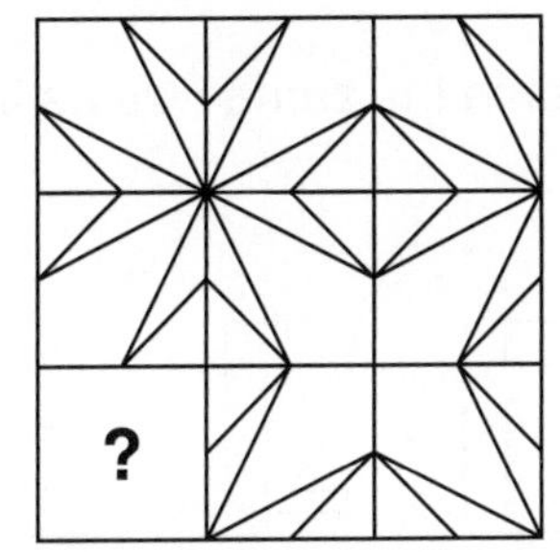

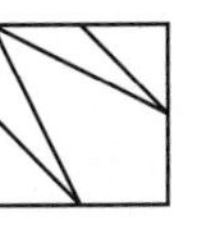

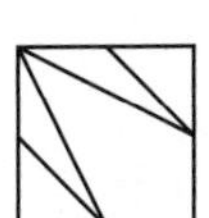 a

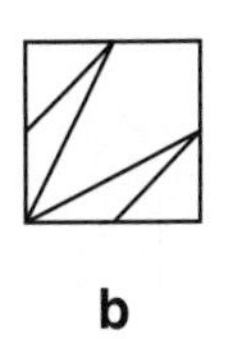 b

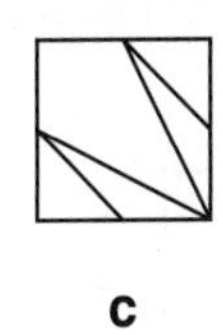 c

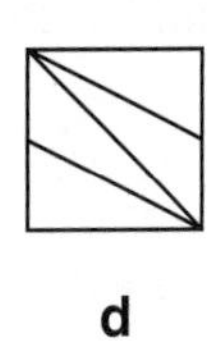 d

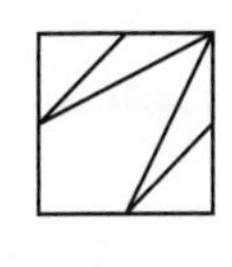 e

33

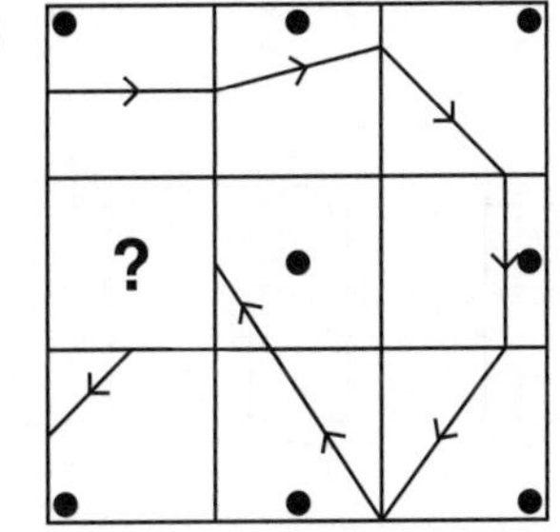

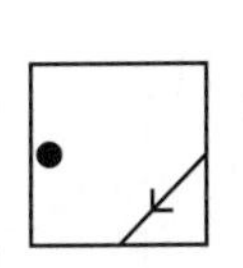 a

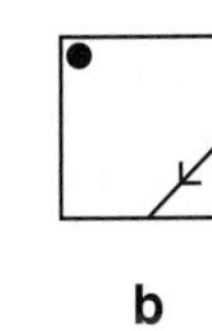 b

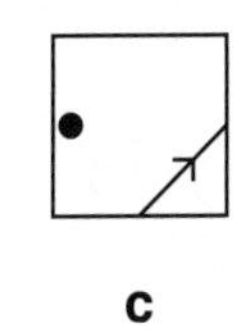 c

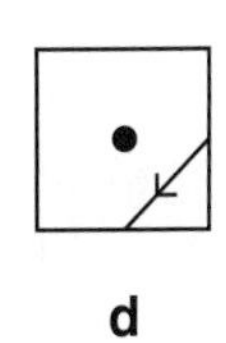 d

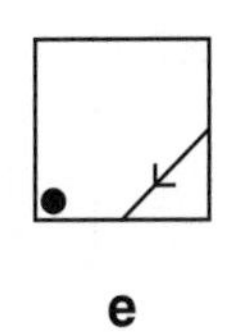 e

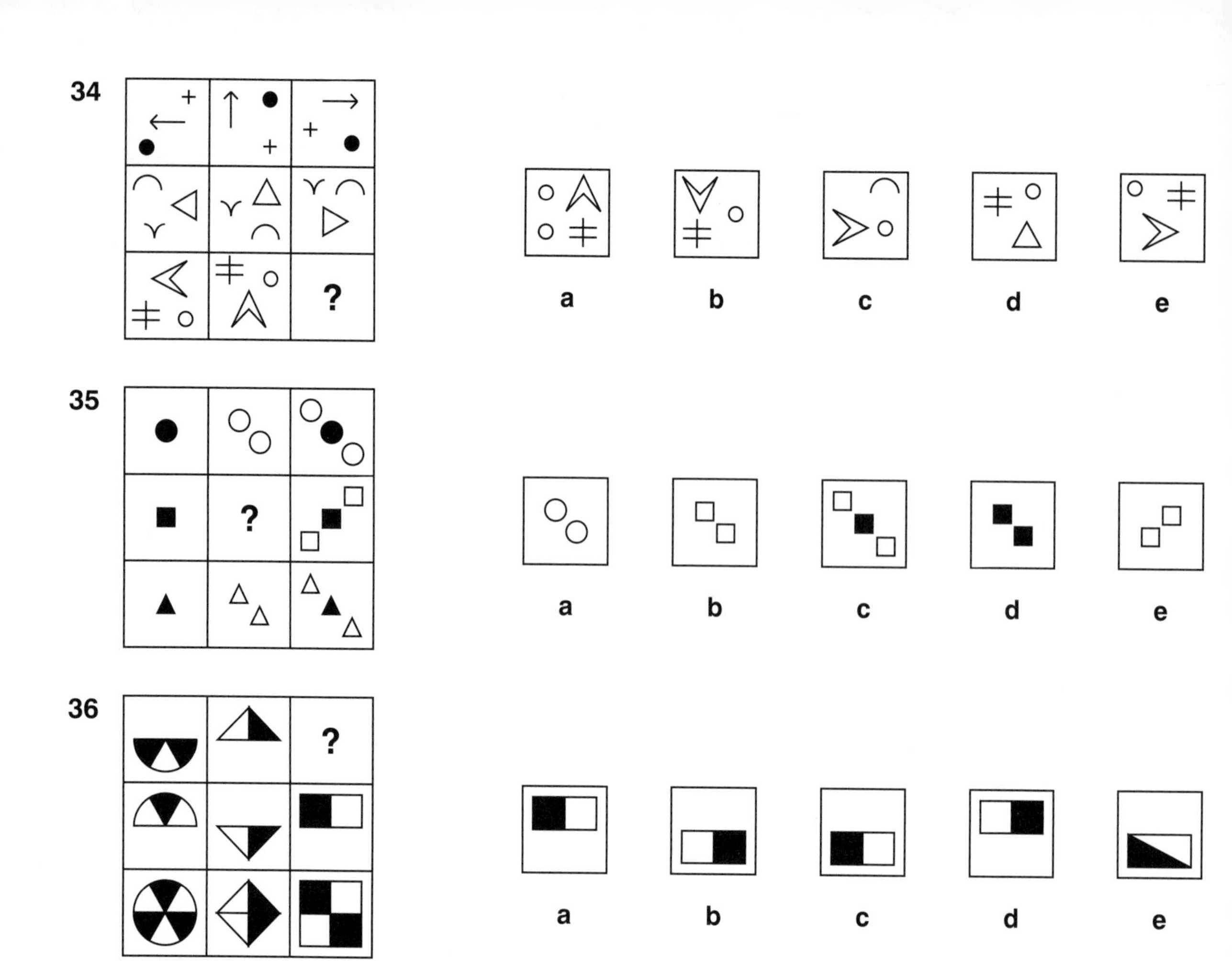

B3 Which shape or pattern on the right completes the second pair in the same way as the first pair? Circle the letter.

Example

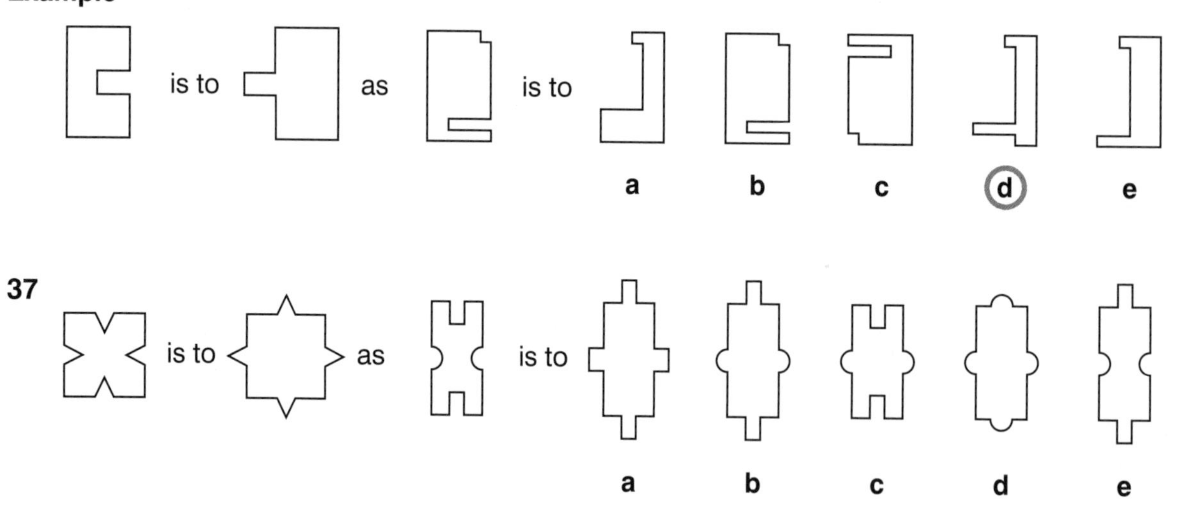

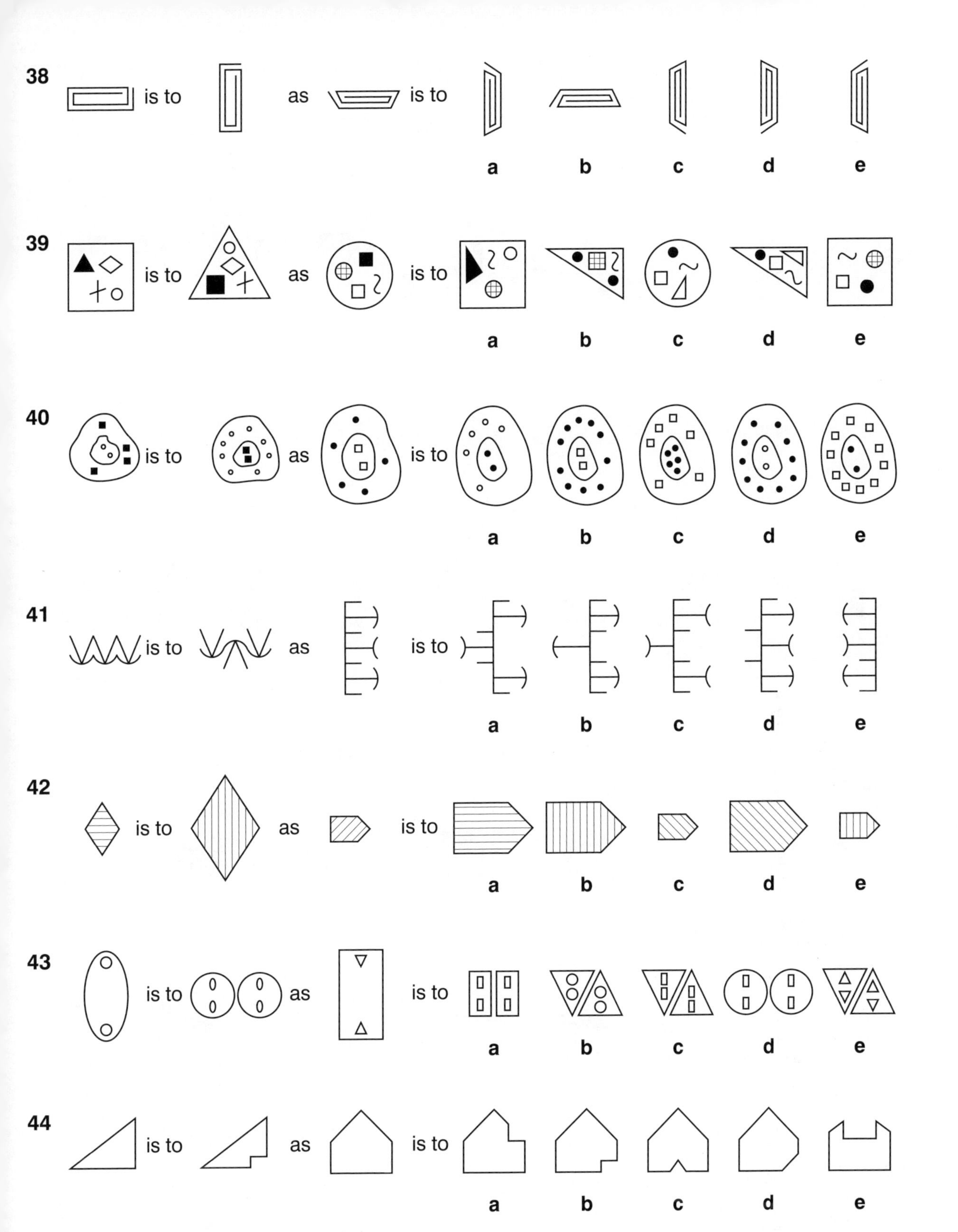
38
is to
as
is to
a
b
c
d
e
39
is to
as
is to
a
b
c
d
e
40
is to
as
is to
a
b
c
d
e
41
is to
as
is to
a
b
c
d
e
42
is to
as
is to
a
b
c
d
e
43
is to
as
is to
a
b
c
d
e
44
is to
as
is to
a
b
c
d
e

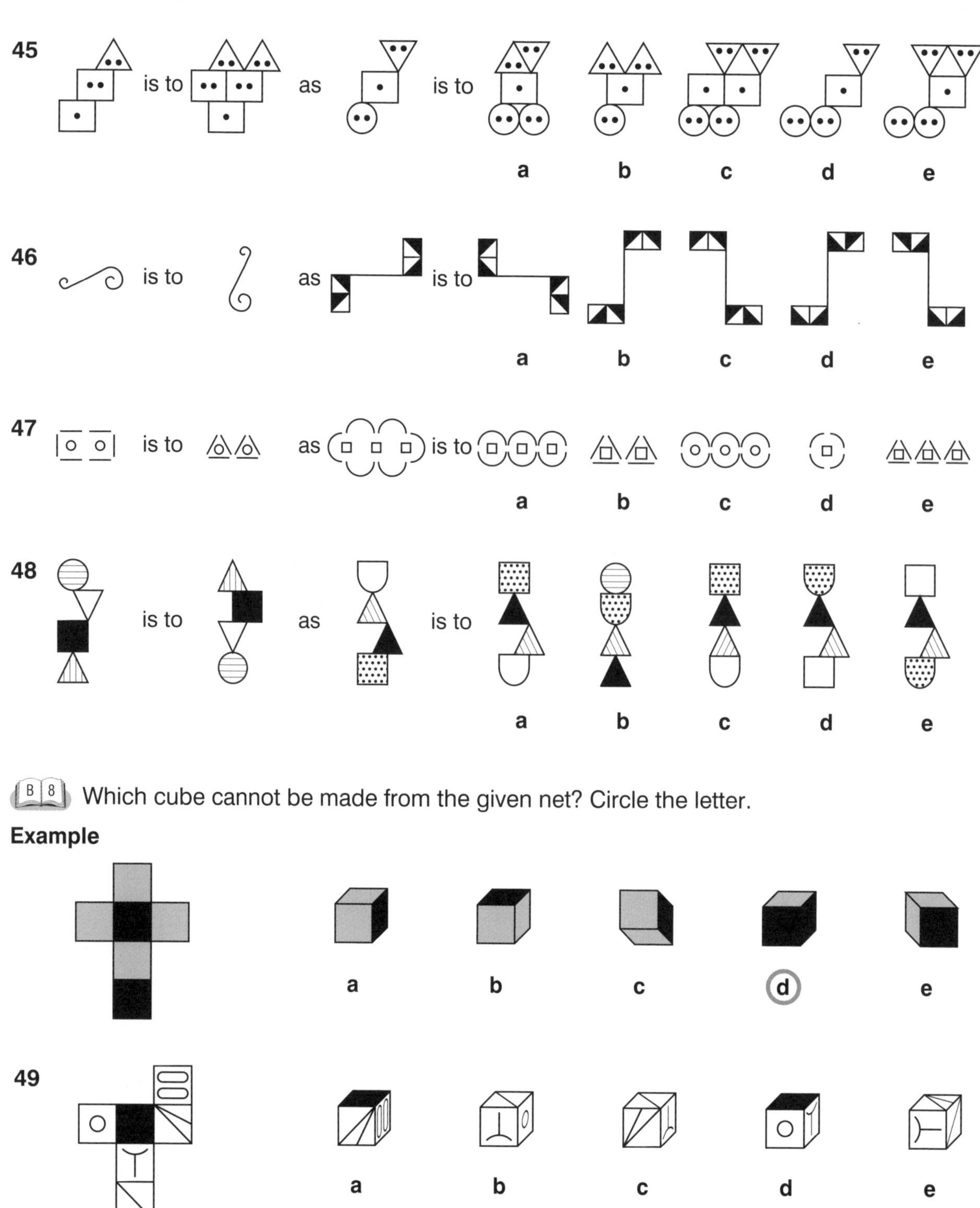

B 8 Which cube cannot be made from the given net? Circle the letter.

Example

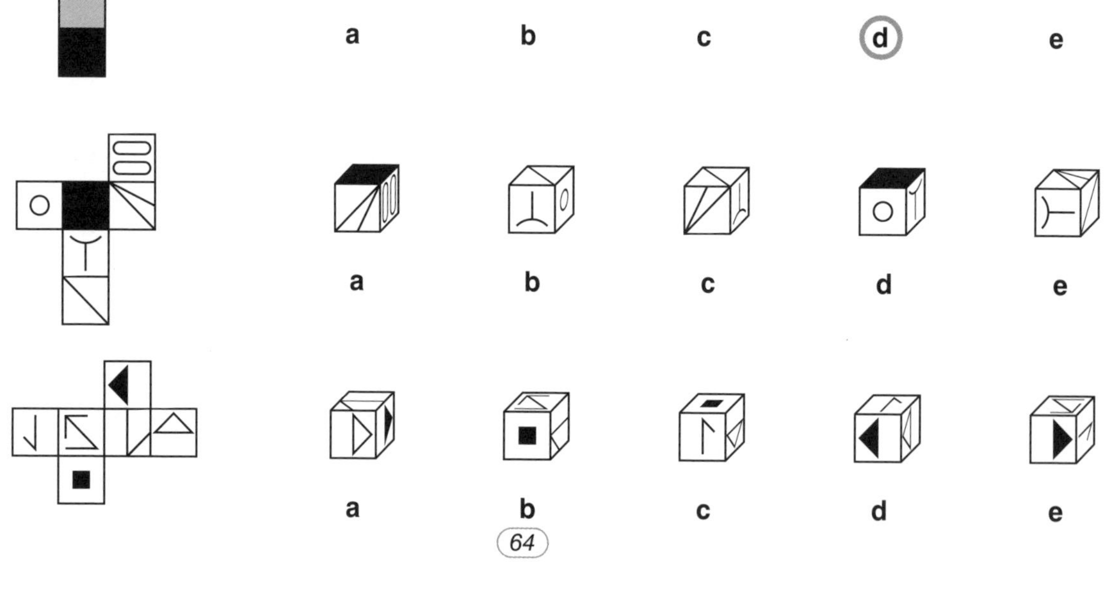

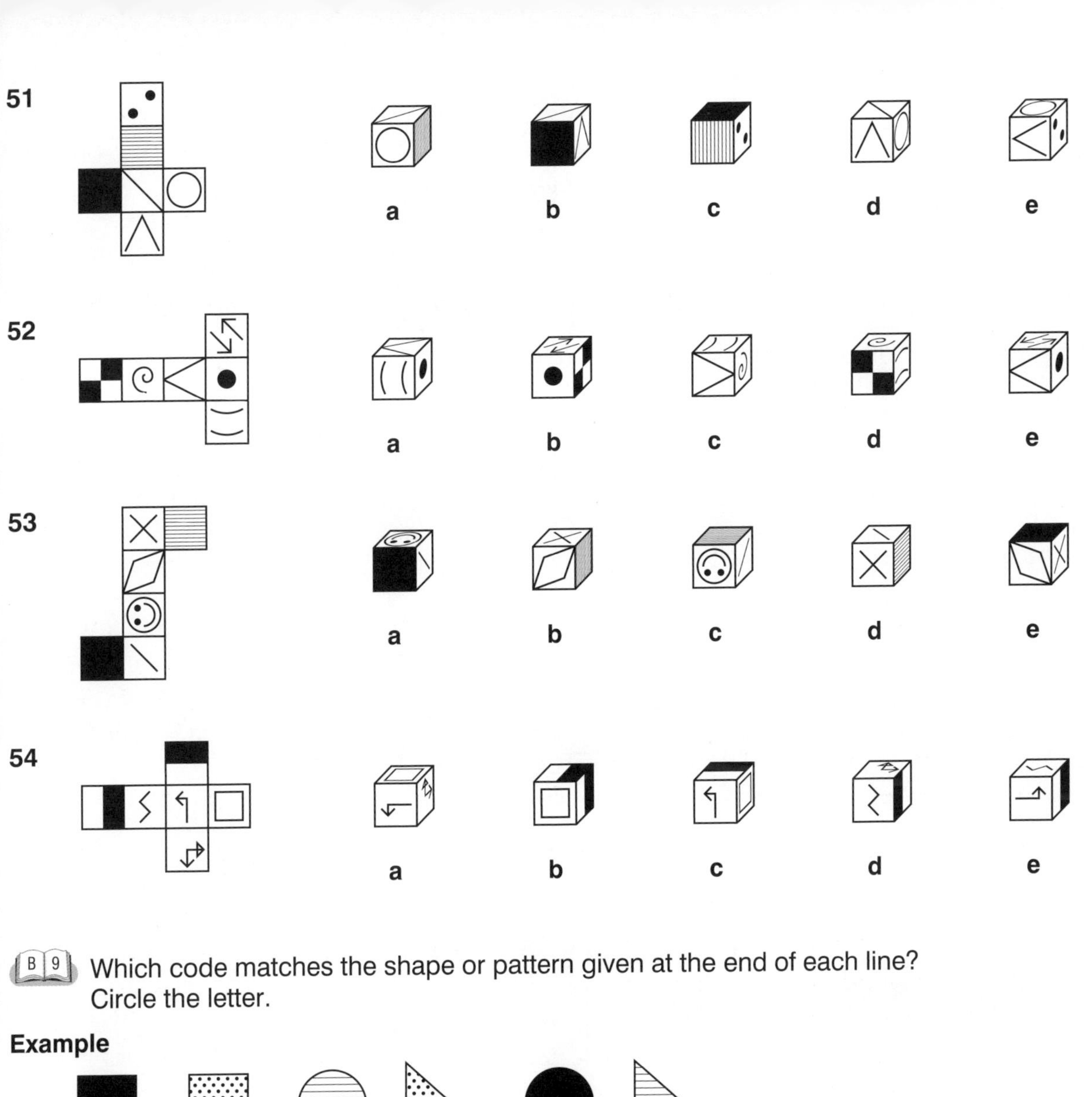

B 9 Which code matches the shape or pattern given at the end of each line?
Circle the letter.

Example

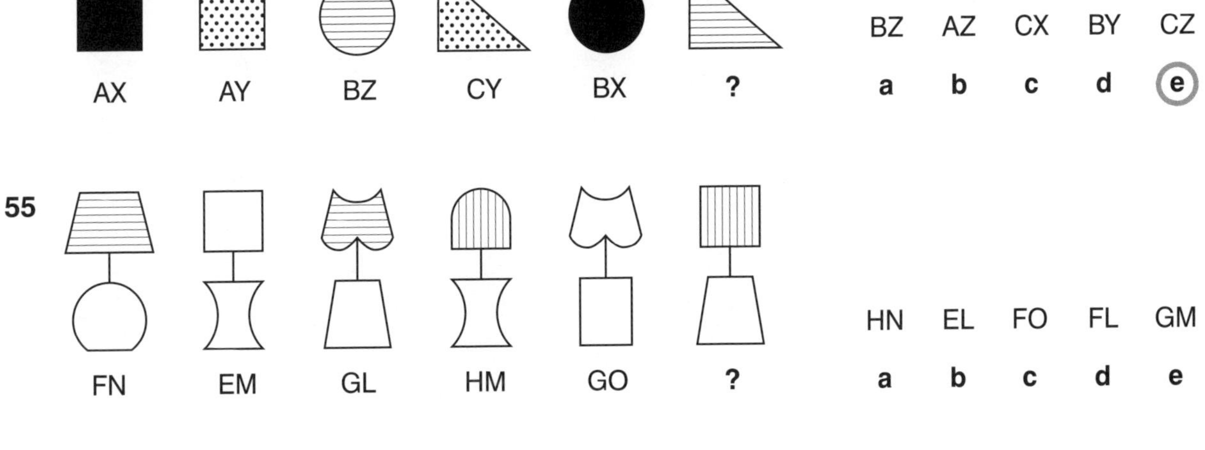

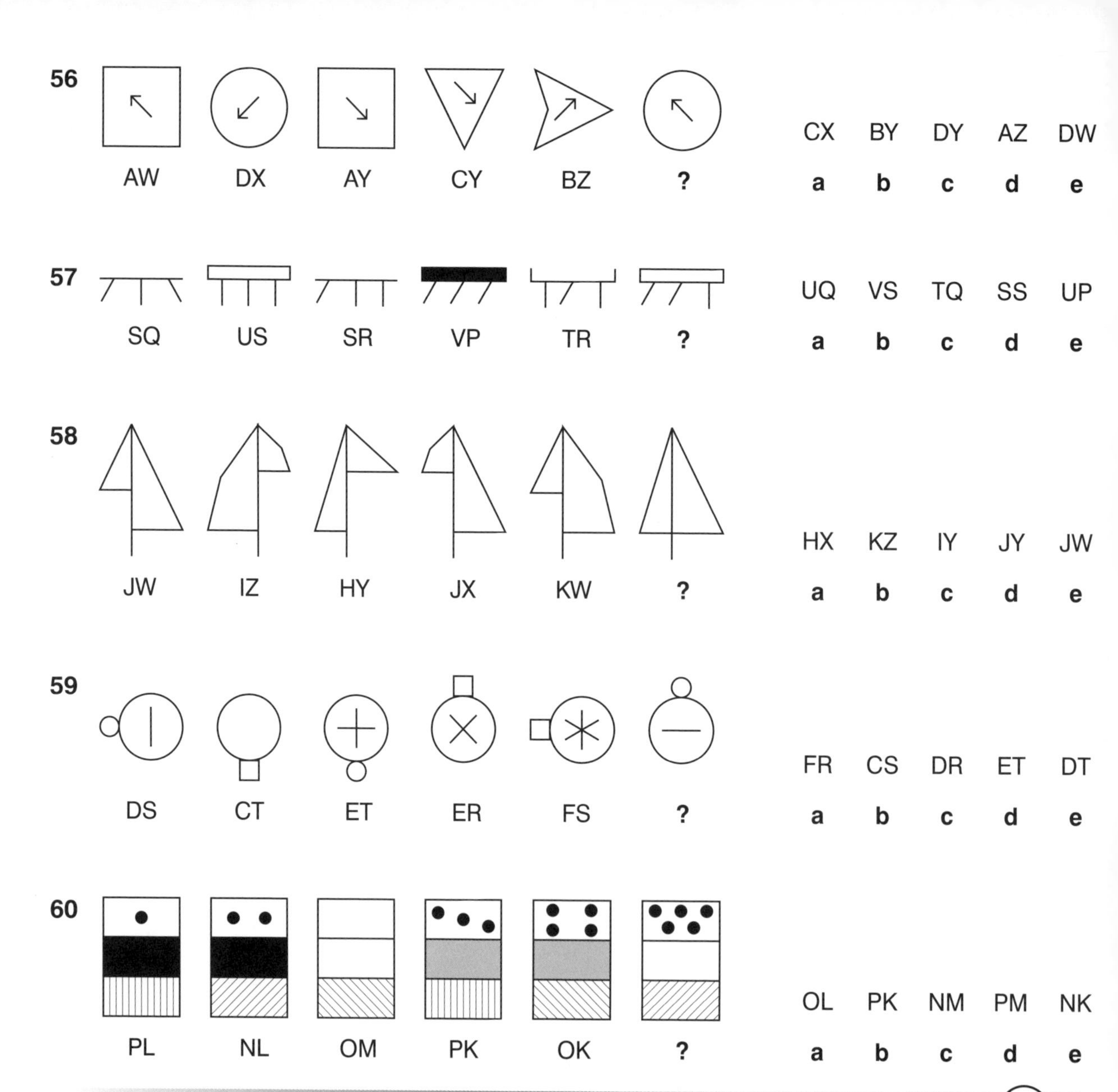

Now go to the Progress Chart to record your score! **Total** ◯ **60**

Progress Chart Non-verbal Reasoning Assessment Papers 11⁺–12⁺ years Book 2

Total marks	Paper 1	Paper 2	Paper 3	Paper 4	Paper 5	Paper 6	Percentage
60							100%
57							
54							90%
51							85%
48							80%
45							
42							70%
39							
36							60%
33							
30							50%
27							
24							40%
21							
18							30%
15							
12							20%
9							
6							10%
3							
0							0%
	1	2	3	4	5	6	
Date							

When you've finished the book use the Next Step Planner